STEPPING AWAY FROM TRADITION

Stepping Away from Tradition

CHILDREN'S BOOKS
OF THE
TWENTIES AND THIRTIES

———————————— ✳ ————————————

PAPERS FROM A SYMPOSIUM

EDITED BY Sybille A. Jagusch

CHIEF, CHILDREN'S LITERATURE CENTER

LIBRARY OF CONGRESS · WASHINGTON

1988

Library of Congress Cataloging-in-Publication Data

Stepping away from tradition.

   Four papers presented at a symposium held at the Library
of Congress on Nov. 15, 1984, sponsored by the Children's
Literature Center and the Center for the Book in the
Library of Congress.
   Bibliography: p.
   Includes index.
   Supt. of Docs. no.:   LC   1.2:St4/2/988
   Contents: For children, with love and profit / John
Tebbel — Designing children's books / Abe Lerner —
Literary and social aspects of children's books of the
twenties and thirties / Anne MacLeod — [etc.]
   1. Children's literature—Publishing—United States—
History—20th century—Congresses.   2. Children—United
States—Books and reading—History—20th century—
Congresses.   3. Children's literature, American—History
and criticism—Congresses.   4. Libraries, Children's—
United States—History—20th century—Congresses.
I. Jagusch, Sybille A.   II. Children's Literature Center
(Library of Congress)   III. Center for the Book.
Z479.S787   1988   070.5'0973   88-600349
ISBN 0-8444-0620-1

Papers from a symposium on
children's literature of the 1920s and 1930s
that took place at the Library of Congress,
November 15, 1984

Supported in part by the Daniel J. and Ruth F. Boorstin
Publications Fund

Book designed by Abe Lerner

CONTENTS

*

FOREWORD

*

The Library of Congress is pleased to publish these four papers about children's books in the 1920s and 1930s that were presented at the Library on November 15, 1984. Ninety guests from throughout the country gathered to hear them and to celebrate the accomplishments of the book people whose energy and idealism in those decades gave the American children's book a distinct identity. The symposium was sponsored by the Children's Literature Center and the Center for the Book in the Library of Congress, two small, catalytic offices concerned with the reading, writing, and promotion of books. Funds for the program and for this publication were provided through private contributions to the Center for the Book and by the Daniel J. and Ruth F. Boorstin Publications Fund.

In this technological age, it is easy to forget that books, reading, and the written word are important parts of our heritage. Moreover, our book culture has helped shape our society. These essays are a powerful reminder of an important American tradition.

JOHN Y. COLE
Director
The Center for the Book
in the Library of Congress

INTRODUCTION

*

Each fall since its opening in 1963, the Children's Literature Center of the Library of Congress has conducted a program commemorating Children's Book Week. Past programs have featured such events as public lectures by authors and panel discussions.

Children's Book Week originated as part of a campaign launched by the Boy Scouts of America in 1912 to heighten the interest of its members in reading. Seven years later, the first formal Children's Book Week was celebrated nationally from November 10 to 15. Since then, each year, and always in November, Children's Book Week has been marked throughout the United States in a variety of ways, by programs highlighting children's books and stressing the pleasures and benefits of reading. Booksellers, librarians, teachers, parents— all whose interests extend to the world of children's books—have taken up its cause.

As the Library of Congress enters its third decade of presenting commemorative programs for this occasion, the Children's Literature Center, in conjunction with the Center for the Book, has chosen to remember the creativity of children's books of the twenties and thirties, a veritable golden age. The period was a time when children's book leaders initiated new developments within the publishing industry and pushed the American children's book further toward its own distinctive and attractive identity.

When Louise Seaman Bechtel (1894–1985) became the first children's book editor in the United States in 1919, at the Macmillan Company, a new field opened up. Other publishing houses were quick to follow the lead and find children's editors of their own. Bechtel and her colleagues, pioneers all, were hard working, idealistic, energetic, and willing to experiment. Open to new ideas, they imported innovations from abroad. Newly arrived foreign artists were put to work, and native writers and illustrators were encouraged to new heights of creativity.

Children's books of the period reflected this dynamism. Thematically and artistically, the books were both more exciting and more oriented to the child than ever before. Truly, as Bechtel remembers, there had never been such a variety to choose from.

If the bookmaking of these years, as Louise Seaman Bechtel wrote in *Books in Search of Children* (Macmillan, 1969), "stepped away from its tradition," it also forged new traditions that have continued into the present. An example of the strength, beauty, and endurance of children's bookmaking in those crucial years is reflected in the strong, clean cover design of the lion drawn by Clement Hurd as well as in the other illustrations I have chosen for this book.

Together the essays presented here document the Library's twenty-first program in honor of Children's Book Week, and they provide a valuable first-hand account of key books, authors, illustrators, publishers, and librarians of the twenties and thirties who contributed so much to making this period one that truly stepped away from tradition.

John Tebbel's account of book publishing for children in the twenties and thirties gives us insight into the prominent figures of those decades as well as an overall view of the types of books and series which were offered. Abe Lerner, in his reminiscences of his days as book designer for the Viking Press, provides a first-hand account of the day-to-day scene in the children's book departments of major publishing houses in the 1930s. Abe Lerner is still practicing his art today, and to my great pleasure, he was willing to design this book, applying his sense of history and craftsmanship to make it distinctive and "pleasant to hold."

Anne McLeod explores the genteel traditions and sensibilities of children's books of the 1920s, whose central themes nevertheless emphasized social mobility, achievement, and materialism. Subject matter in the 1930s, on the other hand, dealt with the familial relationship, emphasizing childhood years and episodic events in a child's life. To conclude, Mildred Batchelder, preeminent children's librarian, provides a comprehensive account of the practitioners in the field of children's librarianship during these two decades.

SYBILLE A. JAGUSCH
Chief
Children's Literature Center

STEPPING AWAY FROM TRADITION

———————*———————

For Children, with Love and Profit:
Two Decades of Book
Publishing for Children

CHILDREN, as we all know, took a very long time to be recognized as human beings. The medievalists have told us of the cold world they once lived in—young adults, so to speak, at five or six, deprived for the most part of what we came to believe later was an essential part of growth—childhood. In early America, children's literature was full of role models that seem bizarre today—impossibly good boys and girls who could count themselves happiest if they died at an early age, as many did, and were transported to the pure joys of heaven, safe from a sinful temporal world.

For much of the early nineteenth century, in fact, children were *lectured* to in books, rather than entertained, until slowly the world of fantasy and myth was opened to them, and in time came books which told of other children who had exciting adventures, lived lives like their own, or inhabited another world. *Little Black Sambo* (1933), for instance, may be decried as racist today, but for millions of children in the rural North it was a harmless introduction to the idea that there were people of a different color in the world, people otherwise no different than they were.

In spite of the appearance of volumes acknowledged now as classics—*Alice, Robinson Crusoe,* and many others—children's books were at best a sideline with publishers until the 1920s. Their publication lacked any kind of organization or direction, appearing often to be the result of an urge for quick profit rather than a serious attempt to enrich the lives of child readers. On publication lists, these volumes appeared with the general titles, and were not considered as a separate category. Only Frederick Leypoldt, who was the first to record book production systematically (which he did in his magazine *Publishers Weekly,* which began publication in 1873) took the trouble to compile separate book lists of children's reading.

All this began to change in 1919, however, when Children's Book Week was inaugurated. Its origins were as early as 1912, when the Boy Scouts of America decided to place greater emphasis on reading for boys and delegated Franklin K. Mathiews, chief scout librarian at national headquarters in New York, to see what could be done. Mathiews began by surveying the field to find out what boys were reading. What he discovered dismayed him. It appeared no one was doing anything to bring about better distribution of books to boys, or by implication, to girls either.

Seeking to make contact with the publishing world, he arranged an invitation from Louis Keating, chairman of the American Booksellers Association (ABA) program committee, to speak before the 1913 annual convention at the Hotel Astor in New York on the subject of "Books as Merchandise or Something More." Mathiews's speech was on a rather high moral plane. He told the booksellers: "I am not expecting that you gentlemen should stop the sale of all bad books, but you can surely slow them up some and can increase the sale of better books."[1] He made such an impression that the first book week in the industry was designated in November of that year. It was called "Safety First Book Week," and in conjunction with it, a small catalog of "Books Boys Like Best" was issued by Mathiews through the *Publishers Weekly (PW)* office. Fifty thousand copies were distributed. Mathiews also made an arrangement with Grosset & Dunlap to establish a Boy Scout Library to market as reprints what were considered the best of the original editions. In 1914, another book week was organized called "Good Book Week," with another catalog distributed to seventy-five thousand people.

There was a hiatus during the war years, and then in 1919, Mathiews was asked to address the ABA convention again. It was a speech that summarized what had been done in the movement and what he himself had learned about it in his travels around the country. Fresh interest was stirred, and Frederic Melcher (1879–1963), who had just become managing editor of *PW* and was ABA secretary as well, proposed a resolution, which was passed, to organize a national "Children's Book Week," extending the original concept to girls as well as boys and to younger children of both sexes. The ABA's executive committee did the organizing and the first Children's Book Week took place that year, from November 10 to November 15, 1919.

The ABA committee appointed to promote the new movement, with Melcher as chairman and Mathiews as vice-chairman, was replete with names later to be distinguished. There was F. Brett Stokes, head of his own house, Maxwell Aley, then a Harper editor and later a noted agent; Anne Carroll Moore, of the New York Public Library; and Harry Maule and Cedric Crowell, both just beginning their careers, from Doubleday. With the help of a five-thousand-dollar fund collected from the publishers, they outlined a program for the first year and produced the initial slogan, "More Books in the Home." A syllabus advising how to conduct a Children's Book Week was mailed to a list of four thousand, and Mathiews himself spent a month traveling through the West and Northwest to spread the gospel. Anne Carroll Moore's help proved to be of special value. Her name was closely associated with children's reading and reading movements in general, and she was extremely persuasive with educational leaders and librarians in gaining their cooperation.

The first Children's Book Week was considered a success, although the number of participating communities was small compared with what it would be in later years. In 1920, Marion Humble, executive secretary of the newly formed National Association of Book Publishers, and former publicity secretary of the Detroit Public Library, was placed in charge of the program.

These details about the origins of Children's Book Week are given at the risk of rehearsing the familiar, not only because of the movement's long-range significance but also because it was the immediate, powerful factor which changed the general attitude of publishers toward this category of book—and they came to it a little reluctantly. Since the first Children's Book Week had occurred during the busy holiday season, many of them found it hard to believe it had made any difference in total sales, even though they thought the movement was "a good thing."

Their general attitude was reflected in the speech made to the 1919 convention of the American Library Association (ALA) by Franklin S. Hoyt, of Houghton Mifflin's educational department, who spoke from the publishers' viewpoint about the difficulty of producing books for children, in words which have an astonishingly contemporary ring.

As a result of the "highly stimulating environment in which they live," said Hoyt, children "become accustomed to the sensational, rather highly seasoned, unreflective type of reading presented in juvenile magazines, and represented by the movie plot. The older type of classic literature, therefore, has lost much of its former appeal, and the author and publisher who wish to provide children with books which are both wholesome and attractive have a difficult undertaking. . . ."

Then Hoyt elaborated on a theme that would be argued for some time to come in the children's book field. Fairy tales had to be discounted, he said, because the world was now so filled with miraculous occurrences. Stories every morning in the newspapers made fiction seem tame and unattractive to many children, making them prime candidates for books about the wonders of the world in which they lived. An increasing number of them were interested in birds and nature study, Hoyt went on, and so could be guaranteed to read eagerly the works of writers like Dallas Lore Sharp (1870–1929), John Burroughs (1837–1921), and Ernest Thompson Seton (1860–1946). Boys were especially interested in books on electricity and the creations of science, he said—and he heard no rebuttals about stereotyping.

But there was a problem. There is always a problem in publishing, and if it is not distribution, it is what Hoyt said bothered him most—the rising cost of manufacturing. (Remember, this is 1919.) Only a few years ago, the man from Houghton Mifflin recalled, a publisher would be justified in bringing out a book for children of the standard twelve-month type, with a projected sale of 2,000 copies the first year and a continuing sale thereafter of 100 or 200 copies annually. Now, however, it was not good economics to publish a book that would sell fewer than 5,000 the first year and 500 thereafter. A profitable backlist item would have to sell several hundred copies annually to justify its continuance. He noted the increase in artists' fees, and the already high cost of color, which he considered prohibitive, predicting that elaborately illustrated children's books in color would disappear. So much for expert opinion. Exactly the opposite occurred, of course. As for prices, Hoyt added, children's books for libraries that had once ranged from seventy-five cents to $1.25 a copy were now listed at $1.00 and $1.50, and further increases could be expected.

Publishers in general were not dismayed by these cautionary words. Children's Book Week alone had been a tremendous stimulus, and it was clear to them that something major was occurring in their business. Other factors were at work too. Children's book departments in public libraries were by then well developed and had their separate quarters, and librarians had been trained to work in them. Branch libraries were expanding, furthermore, and a new kind of school library had come upon the scene, providing for general reading as well as making regular schoolbooks available.

Another stimulus was the establishment of the John Newbery Medal in 1922. The award originated at the ALA convention of 1921, where the ubiquitous Fred Melcher offered the idea to the delegates, volunteering to supply the medal himself, and suggesting it be named to honor Newbery, the London bookseller who was probably the first to give specific attention to the reading interests of children. The first winner was Hendrik Willem Van Loon, for *The Story of Mankind* (New York: Boni & Liveright, 1921).

Frederic Melcher, Carolyn W. Field, Barbara Cooney, Elizabeth George Speare, and Elizabeth Nesbitt at the presentation of the Newbery and Caldecott Awards at the Sheraton Plaza Hotel, Washington, D.C., on June 23, 1959. Courtesy of Mildred Batchelder.

17

CHILDREN'S
BOOK EDITORS
AND
CHILDREN'S
LIBRARIANS

Observing the rapidly increasing interest in children's books, publishers took the logical next step and began to organize separate departments for them. That proved to be one of the most remarkable developments of the decade in publishing, and it resulted in an extraordinary upsurge of vitality and quality in children's books. It was directly related to the emergence of women as an important force in publishing, as they at last shook off at least some of the restrictions which had kept them largely in clerical or mechanical jobs. They still had a long way to go, but women found in the rise of American books for children, and the consequent establishment of children's book departments in publishing houses, an opportunity to better themselves.

Examining the phenomenon of the new department in the *Horn Book* in 1936, Bertha Mahoney Miller (1882–1969) traced its origins to elements in the American heritage clamoring for expression, to the development of children's rooms in public libraries, and to the emergence of an outstanding group of women editors. Louise Seaman Bechtel (1894–1985), who became editor of children's books at Macmillan in 1919, and May Massee (1881–1966), appointed to the same job for Doubleday, Doran in 1922, were the stars of the show, but others soon followed. Of these two pioneers, Bertha Miller wrote: "They brought a new force into the publishing of children's books. Their sympathetic understanding and full appreciation of the creative personality; their enthusiastic succor and protection of their authors and illustrators is the spirit shown by some editors of an earlier and more leisurely time. . . ."[2]

These two pioneering women deserve a closer look. After her education at Packer Institute (in Brooklyn, New York) and at Vassar, Louise Seaman began by teaching and working in playgrounds and settlements. After three years of teaching in a private school in New Haven and doing some graduate work at Yale, she decided to go into publishing. Following in the footsteps of an earlier pioneer, Jessie Reed, who was head of Macmillan's educational department, she bearded the formidable George Brett, head of that house, in his office in the old red Macmillan Building on Fourth Avenue, and boldly asked him for a job. As he had done with Reed, Brett gave her one in the advertising department; later she moved to the education division. As it happened, Brett had been thinking about establishing a children's book department, and when he made the move, he named Louise Seaman as manager.

She brought more than the usual experience to her job, having handled accounts as a regular salesperson for the house, and having visited all its branch offices. Consequently, she was able not only to choose and plan books but to supervise their manufacture, illustration, and decoration. Among her accomplishments as an editor was the launching of the Work and Play books; the publication of an Italian *Pinocchio*, printed in Italy from the original plates; the inauguration of the Little Library, with authors like Daudet, Rossetti, and Ruskin; and the introduction of a line of fifty-cent classics, including *The Ugly Duckling, Hansel and Gretel,* and *The Pied Piper.* She gave talks on books at women's clubs, Parent-Teacher Association meetings, libraries, and bookshops, and she was one of the first to realize what could be done with radio. For two years she read to children for an hour each week on the air. The catalogs of the books that she put out for Macmillan were such works of art that they were reviewed in the newspapers, along with the new books.

May Massee, Miss Seaman's counterpart at Doubleday, was born and brought up in Chicago. She studied at the University of Wisconsin Library School and was children's librarian in the Buffalo Public Library before she left to edit the *A.L.A. Booklist.* One day in 1922, she was lunching at the Blackstone Hotel in Chicago with Sam Everett, vice-president of Doubleday, Page, when he asked her for suggestions about the new children's book department he was planning, and particularly whom he might hire to manage it. After she had named several people, Everett gave her the classic, although mythical line, "Why don't you speak for yourself, John?" She accepted at once.

Soon after she came to Doubleday, at another luncheon conversation with a friend, she was talking enthusiastically about her ideas for children's books. "They must have color, beauty, better illustrations, type, paper, but most of all real color," she said. A man sitting nearby, smoking his pipe, was listening and broke in: "I want to make a picture book like that, an ABC book for Bedelia Jane. And I want to make all the wood blocks."

"All right," May Massee told him, "we'll make one." An ABC book with block print illustrations—in color.[3]

The man was C. B. Falls (1874–1960), and the *ABC Book* he created became Massee's first new book. Published in November 1923, it had sold seven thousand copies by Christmas, with three subsequent reprints, and was a perennial seller for years afterward.

That was only a small sample of the imagination, vitality, and intelligence that May Massee brought to children's book publishing—attributes that caused her to be regarded by many people in the industry as the foremost editor in her field, although Louise Seaman's admirers would have disputed that.

One of the most important contributions made by these two women was in design. Before them, picture books of distinction had been rare in American children's publishing. The volumes of Kate Greenaway (1846–1901), Randolph Caldecott (1836–1886), Walter Crane (1845–1915), and Leslie Brooke (1862–1940) were imported from England and admired, while America could boast of Howard Pyle (1853–1911), among others. But these artists who decided the format their books would take were isolated figures. May Massee and Louise Seaman changed that and in the process gave to the designers of children's books an importance they had not known previously.

In fact, taste and intelligence were the hallmark of nearly all the women who came to be managers of the new children's book departments in the twenties. Many of them stayed in publishing for years, and a few made reputations in other parts of the business. Virginia Kirkus, for example, who became department editor at Harper (although not the first one) after teaching in progressive schools and serving for years in the editorial departments of *McCall's* and *Pictorial Review*, went on from Harper's to found and conduct the reviewing service that still bears her name.

By 1926, the trend toward establishing children's book departments in publishing houses was in full swing. Macmillan; Doubleday; Stokes; Harcourt; Longmans, Green; Dutton; and Harper had committed themselves fully, and others were experimenting. McBride joined the list in 1928 with Carroll Wilford, well-known for her work in the children's department of the White Plains Public Library, as manager. Almost at the same time, Alfred Knopf announced that he had decided to place the borzoi imprint on the products of a new children's book department; previously he had published only a few books for children. Knopf announced that he would start with a few titles already in the catalog, including Walter de la Mare's anthologies, Hudson's *Little Boy Lost*, Belloc's *Cautionary Rhymes*, Barbara Folette's books, a new Mother Goose, and the *Arabian Nights*. Marion Fiery was hired away from Dutton to head the newly formed Knopf department.

20

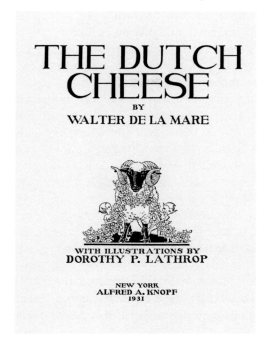

The Dutch Cheese,
by Walter De La Mare,
with illustrations by
Dorothy P. Lathrop
(New York: Alfred A. Knopf,
© 1931). Reproduced by permission
of Alfred A. Knopf, Inc.

Other changes were taking place in children's books. Comparing those of 1923 with the books available in 1880 or 1885, *PW* was struck by the sharp contrasts.[4] In the late nineteenth century, it noted, storybooks had been profoundly influenced by excellent magazines for children such as *St. Nicholas* (1873–1940, 1943), *Harper's Round Table* (1895–99), formerly *Harper's Young People* (1879–95), and *Wide Awake* (1875–1893). Many volumes from that era were still in demand in the twenties, along with the British imports. But now new artists were being developed in America, and picture books had become much richer and more diversified in spite of the high cost of color work. A broadening market and large sales made the investment worthwhile for publishers.

Entirely new was the tremendous interest among children in books on popular science, invention, and nature. In the 1920s, such volumes were already a major part of the market, and the market was growing rapidly every year. Significant, too, was the availability from other countries of children's books in English translation— wide selections from the folklore and fairy tales of virtually every

21

nation producing such a literature, as well as translations of such books as *The Wonderful Adventures of Nils* and *Pinocchio*.

All these developments were given impetus by the children's library movement in public libraries. Its leaders had created the demand for new editions and reprints of the best literature of past generations, and then had turned that demand toward encouraging the production of new books. They represented a body of organized opinion, backed by purchasing power, that had a major effect on the development of children's literature and the publishing of it.

MARKETING
CHILDREN'S
BOOKS: NEW
METHODS,
NEW FORMS,
NEW ARTISTS

Publishers were also taking advantage of the fresh selling outlets opening up. In 1921, Harper made special efforts to interest toy dealers in handling children's books, offering a Harper Library for Boys made up in sets of ten, ranging from *Robinson Crusoe* down to G. A. Henty and Ralph Heyliger. The books were boxed in attractive cartons, and a steel section to hold them was given with each set. As the customer purchased another group of books, another steel section was automatically added and fitted together to make a bookcase. A set, with steel section to go along, cost fifteen dollars. There was a similar library for girls. The plan was merchandised from Harper's new promotion headquarters at 130 West Forty-second Street, from which the firm was still pushing its famous "Bubble Book" nursery phonograph.

Picture books were another category that publishers were beginning to exploit in the twenties. American productions in this field had lagged behind European imports for years, and trade observers believed that domestic picture books were in a rut, although American houses had proven to be ingenious in combining toys or cutouts with books. The volumes, however, were usually done either in black and white or in four-color process plate. Volland books were the biggest success in this market, at seventy-five cents to $1.25, nearly equaled by the big picture books turned out by Saalfield, Sully, and a few others.

It was this field that Macmillan entered in 1927 with a new series called The Happy Hour Books, of forty-eight pages, in black-and-flat color, five and a quarter inches square, bound in board, Singer sewn, with an all-over full-color jacket that was a duplicate of the binding design. The first dozen titles were printed in arresting color combinations, and they sold for fifty cents.

Needless to say, this series was Louise Seaman's inspiration. She had surveyed the cheap book field and concluded that there was a place for new and artistic picture books for small children. Her first choices for the series were familiar, competitive titles, but few of them existed in separate color books. They constituted what could be called a standard list of children's publishing in the twenties: *Wee Willie Winkie, Three Little Pigs, Little Black Sambo, Hansel and Gretel, Jack and the Beanstalk, The Steadfast Tin Soldier, Humpty Dumpty, The Three Billy Goats, Chicken Little, The Ugly Duckling, The Bremen Band,* and *The Pied Piper.* If it were possible to compile an equivalent standard list today, few, if any, of these 1927 books would appear on it, and one, *Little Black Sambo,* could not be published at all without protest. Conceivably, *Chicken Little* could be issued as a right-wing satire.

The *Happy Hour Books* were added to a Macmillan children's book department that already included its Children's Classic Series, based on original editions of *Alice in Wonderland* and *Grimm's Fairy Tales;* and its modern Little Library, built on the original *Rose and the Ring* and *Memoirs of a London Doll.*

Some of the new developments in the picture book field had their American origins in McLoughlin Bros., the earliest publishing house in the nation devoted to children's books alone, and makers of the first picture books for them. This firm had completed a century of publishing in 1928. Among the nursery books of the twenties, McLoughlin's *ABC Animal Picture Books,* a beautifully illustrated *Mother Goose,* and the Child Activity Series, were among the leaders in the field.

An important new house, begun as a result of the heavy demand for children's books after the First World War—and their short supply before the major trade houses filled the void by establishing their own departments—was Platt & Munk, founded in December 1920. Among its early books which kept on selling year after year were the *Gateway to Story Land* (1925), one of its first productions; the *Brimful Book,* a best-seller for twenty years; and *The Little Engine That Could* (appearing in 1930), whose sales were over a million copies. The houses brought out as many as thirty-eight new titles annually at one point.

The years from 1920 to 1950 have been called a golden age for children's books. Certainly the twenties were a decade of exciting experimentation with new methods and new forms. Along with the

could not go another inch. She tried
and she tried, but her wheels would not
turn.

What were all those good little boys
and girls on the other side of the mountain
going to do without the jolly toys to play
with and the wholesome food to eat?

"Here comes a shiny new engine," said
the little clown who had jumped out of the
train. "Let us ask him to help us."

So all the dolls and toys cried out
together:

"Please, Shiny New Engine, do carry
our train over the mountain. Our engine

has broken down, and the boys and girls
on the other side will have no toys to play
with and no wholesome food to eat unless
you help us."

The Little Engine That Could, *by Watty Piper. Pictures
by Lois L. Lenski. Copyright 1930, copyright renewed © 1957 by Platt &
Munk, Publishers. Reproduced by permission.*

collection and publication of folktales originating in oral as well as
written sources were modern fairy tales. They predominated in
books like Carl Sandburg's *Rootabaga Stories* (1922). Also published
were Margery Bianco's fantasies, the Chinese fairy tales of Arthur
Chrisman, and Irish tales of Anne Casserley.

A. A. Milne's *When We Were Very Young* appeared in 1924, an-
nouncing not only a new poet of childhood but a writer of children's
tales whose *Winnie the Pooh* stories would become twentieth-
century classics and make a name for Dutton, his American publisher. Writers with established reputations in adult books, among
them Elizabeth Madox Roberts and Rachel Field, were also writing
poetry for children, along with such noted poets as Vachel Lindsay,
whose *Johnny Appleseed and Other Poems* was issued in 1928.

Adventure stories were popular. A master of the genre was A. J.
Villiers, whose story of the last clipper ship race around Cape Horn,
Falmouth for Orders, appeared in 1939. Writers of tales with histor-

ical backgrounds entertained children with a kind of book in this field far removed in quality and authenticity from prewar versions of the same events. Elsie Singmaster's *Boy at Gettysburg* (1924) was a popular example, along with the work of new authors, such as Constance Lindsay Skinner.

Recognition of the need of preschool children to have books relating to their everyday experiences produced such writers as Lucy Sprague Mitchell. More and more, it appeared, stories for all ages had an American background, particularly books that dealt with specific regions of the nation, with the stories rising naturally out of their backgrounds. Will James's *Smoky* (1926) was an outstanding example.

Yet children found romantic adventure in stories from other lands as well. Dhan Gopal Mukerji's books and magazine stories gave many children their first sense of the vast Indian subcontinent, and by 1929 there was a lengthy list of books about children in other lands. Among the most popular were the Twins series, written and illustrated by Lucy Fitch Perkins. History also found a fresh life in Hendrik Willem Van Loon's book *The Story of Mankind*, read avidly by young and old alike.

When Lindbergh flew the Atlantic in 1927, his flight touched off not only books by and about him, but a flood of stories for children about aviation, notably Richard Byrd's *Skyward* (1928), concerning his North Pole and transatlantic flights, and *Sky High* (1929), by Eric P. Hodgins and Frederick A. Magoun, the first important history of aviation for young people.

In biographical writing, Theodore Roosevelt was still being published in 1928, with *Diaries of Boyhood and Youth*. Sandburg's *Abe Lincoln Grows Up*, published that same year, gave young Americans a literary, if not always an accurate, view of a national hero. The first of Jeanette Eaton's fine biographies, *A Daughter of the Seine*, was issued in 1929. American picture books were coming into their own during the decade, and it could be safely asserted that this effort was crowned in 1928 with Wanda Gag's *Millions of Cats*.

But it was the artists, as much as the writers, who made the decade of the twenties truly golden. Boris Artzybasheff, then a young and relatively unknown artist, began to draw for the children's market in 1925. In 1928 he conceived a book of his own, using the words of familiar poets and a new technique that mimicked the appearance of wood blocks. This was *The Fairy Shoemaker and Other Poems*. Illustrators, in fact, could turn a primarily adult book into an attractive title for children, as was the case with James Boyd's *Drums*, reissued in 1928 with color illustrations by N. C. Wyeth.

By the end of 1929, *Publishers Weekly* was saying of children's books that they were

> demanding and winning the finest talent creating today. Not only in writing is this true but in illustration and decoration, and in production. The standards are new standards. And the new volumes are colorful and stimulating, as they should be for children. . . . The time is fast passing when children's books were allowed a small space in the corner of a dark basement. The Fifty Books exhibits, which always include a fair number of children's books, the Newbery Award, the recent bookshop ventures that deal exclusively in books for youngsters, and the exhibits of original illustrations for children's books have done much to increase the importance of this branch of publishing.[5]

THE THIRTIES AND THE GREAT DEPRESSION

Paradoxically, it was the great successes of the twenties that were the root cause of the crisis in children's book publishing which occurred in the early thirties. During the booming twenties, the expansion of children's books had been too rapid to endure the economic hardships that came with the Depression. No category of titles had multiplied more rapidly during the golden decade, and now the inevitable reaction occurred as publishers were compelled to reevaluate their operations, including children's book departments. The first result was a rapid decrease in the number of titles published, which meant that the departments themselves were curtailed, and in some cases eliminated. Harper's, for example, whose department was one of the oldest and largest, rescinded its independent status and made it a part of general editorial. That led Virginia Kirkus to leave the firm and found the book reviewing services that made her famous. At Macmillan, Louise Seaman's assistant, Eunice Blake, lost her job, and at Doubleday, the already legendary May Massee lost her junior books department, which was placed under a trade editor, Dorothy Bryant. Knopf gave up its separate children's book department entirely. And Coward-McCann merged its children's books with those of Longmans, Green.

Children's book publishing thus came to a crisis point after a decade of steady growth, during which, ironically, it had shown the way to reach potential markets that were well defined. The women who ran the departments had found ways to not only maintain but improve physical production of their books, using every new process available, working out economies in makeup and layout, and still pricing their products reasonably. It was no accident that a good part of book production experimentation in the twenties had occurred in these departments. Since their directors had to be saleswomen as well as producers of books, they had generated a widespread understanding of what was happening in their field through meetings with librarians and teachers as they traveled across the country.

The crisis of the Depression hurt children's books particularly because many books had been contracted for, involving high production costs, and these projects had to be carried out at a time when money was scarce and when library buying, on which the departments so much depended, had dropped by 25 percent.

To meet the curtailment of purchasing power, children's book editors followed the lead of other trade books and concentrated for a time on finding and selling popular reprints. At the bottom of the Depression, as a result, there had never been a time when so many substantial, beautiful books were available at prices from fifty cents to one dollar. The skills developed in the twenties for making the most tasteful and fullest use of typography and color were now brought to bear on the new problems with striking effect. And in original publishing, there was nothing but admiration in the industry for May Massee, who had come to Viking from Doubleday in 1933 and immediately produced such classics as *The Story about Ping*, illustrated by Kurt Wiese and written by Marjorie Flack, and *The Story of Ferdinand*, by Munro Leaf. Subsequent books she published for Viking won nine Newbery medals and six Caldecotts.

With such editors and methods, the crisis in children's books was short-lived. By the end of 1935, the output of titles had definitely turned upward again, and publishers were exhibiting renewed confidence in the market, on the basis of a slow, steady upturn in sales. To illustrate the dimensions of the previous decline, in 1931 there had been 873 new titles and 245 new editions, and by 1934 the new titles had dropped to 466 and new editions to 135.

One element in the sales increase was the renewed popularity of the fifty-cent book for children. Once that sum had been considered the maximum amount children themselves would spend for a book, and houses had two different kinds of fifty-cent lines for that mar-

THE FIFTY-
CENT BOOK
AND THE
COLORFUL
PICTURE BOOK

27

ket. One was the popular series, such as the Tom Swift, Rover Boys, or Bobbsey Twins stories. The other was the old favorite, printed in large, low-priced editions. By 1935, copyrights on many of the popular books of 1885 had expired, and consequently *Tom Sawyer, Hans Brinker, The Story of a Bad Boy,* and other old favorites became available for reprinting. Publishers had also been looking over the books of the past for reprint material and were now bringing out new editions of *Two Years before the Mast,* Kipling's India stories, and biographies of Kit Carson, Davy Crockett, and other traditional heroes.

Fifty-cent books for children were a continuing phenomenon in the book business. When Edward Stratemeyer, the chief entrepreneur of this popular series kind of fiction, died in May 1930 at age sixty-eight, it was estimated that his books, under various pseudonyms, had sold more than five million copies, and as we all know, they are still selling today in new versions by contemporary writers. A. L. Burt, taking over the Elsie Dinsmore books in 1925, boosted them in the thirties to a renewed popularity, pushing their sales figures into the hundreds of thousands. The belief was that these and the other fifty-cent lines owed their overwhelming success not simply to their low price but to the fact that young readers did the kind of word-of-mouth advertising for them that no publishing house could do.

Stratemeyer was the dominant figure in this field. One of the most enduring contributions was the introduction of Nancy Drew, his last act before his death. She is still alive and well today. Stratemeyer also wrote the Rover Boys series under the pseudonym of Arthur M. Winfield, the Tom Swift series as Victor Appleton, and the Hardy Boys as Franklin W. Dixon—these, among many others. The others included several series for girls; the Honeybunch books, as Helen Louise Thorndike; the Ruth Fielding series, as Alice B. Emerson; the Bobbsey Twins series as Laura Lee Hope; and the Dana Girl series, as Carolyn Keene, whose name, of course, also adorned the Nancy Drew books.

A whole galaxy of writers of fifty-cent series belonged to the Stratemeyer Syndicate. Stratemeyer was the original author of all of them, but in time the load became too great, and he hired writers to take over his many pseudonyms. Some series writers had so many pseudonyms that they could say, as Josephine Chase did, "The only time people will ever know I am a writer will be when I die and they write my obituary."[6] And in truth, only when she died, in 1931 at forty-six, was it known that she had written the Marjorie Dean series, as Pauline Lester; the Grace Harlowe series, as Jessie Graham Flower; the Patsy Carroll and June Allen books, as Grace Gordon; and, displaying her versatility, the Long Trail Boys and Adventure Boys series, as Ames Thompson—to none of which she signed her real name.

Stratemeyer was not without rivals, of course, in the fifty-cent field. Cupples & Leon, one of the major houses in that market, listed about 240 books in twenty-eight series on the backs of the jackets on its fifty-cent books, and added the invitation, "Send for new complete free illustrated catalog." In 1931, this firm alone sold more than a million copies of its serial novels, without any of the usual recommendations or consumer advertising.

If publishers skimped on some of the production details in these books, they spared no expense to make the jackets as attractive as possible, because it was agreed that they were of the greatest importance to such unadvertised items. Child buyers plucked them from racks or tables in department stores, toy shops, small-town corner drugstores, and stationery stores. Consequently the jacket became the principal salesman.

But because thousands of young people who bought the books never saw them in stores, titles were considered important too. These buyers chose from the books listed in the great storehouse catalogs of Sears, Roebuck and Montgomery Ward, as well as in dozens of other catalogs. Grosset & Dunlap's series by Leo Edwards demonstrated how titles could be used to sell books by calling them *The Rose-Colored Cat, The Waltzing Hen, The Galloping Snail, Pedigreed Pickles,* and *The Bob-Tailed Elephant.* Edwards, whose real name was Edward Edson Lee, turned out a veritable flood of volumes from his studio, which he called Storyland, near his cottage on Lake Ripley, Wisconsin. When he wasn't creating heroes named Trigger Berg, Jerry Tood, Andy Blake, Poppy Ott, and Tuffy Bean, he was corresponding with the thousands of boys who formed his fan club, the Freckled Goldfish Club. His chief rival was Percy Keese Fitzhugh, who created such favorites as Tom Slade, Roy Blakely, Pee-Wee Harris, and Westy Martin series.

Whether sold by title, jacket, or both, fifty-cent books were no

longer considered "cheap books," with the connotation of disreput-
ability, as they had once been, but as "stepping stones to literature,"
as Frank Mathiews called them. Mathiews believed that the books
helped children learn to read by paragraphs, not by words and sen-
tences. Nevertheless, these volumes were seldom on librarians' recommended lists, although they could often be found on library
shelves. It was agreed that there was plenty of chaff in the fifty-cent
wheat, but parents and librarians were urged to do more winnowing.

Commercially, there was no argument. Fifty-cent series made up
the largest part of the 22.4 million copies of children's books sold in
1931, or 14.5 percent of all books manufactured. Even the sales of
such best-selling adult authors as Harold Bell Wright, who in his
time had written only one book that sold fewer than a million copies, could not compete with the figures compiled by Stratemeyer
alone, who sold twenty million or more in his lifetime, and the
golden tide continued to roll for decades after his death. Moreover,
many of the characters he created—the Rover Boys, Tom Swift, the
Motor Boys—became national institutions, a part of the language
and culture.

Those who sought to establish the reason for such phenomenal
popularity could point to the single theme underlying all these
books—the total inability of the hero or heroine to fail. Critics
might charge, as they did, that the fifty-cent volumes were overex-
citing to children and led to overstimulation, perhaps permanent, of
the imagination—a quaint idea left over from the nineteenth century. But this pseudoscientific moralizing had no effect whatever on
the popularity of the fifty-cent lines. What eventually killed them
was the growing sophistication of teenagers, who in time suc-
cumbed to such writers of supposedly adult adventures as Edgar
Rice Burroughs and Sax Rohmer.

Fifty-cent books were not the only factor stimulating publishing
for children in the thirties, however. By the middle of the decade, it
was clear that picture books were becoming a major part of the rela-
tive boom which followed the worst of the Depression. In the early
twenties, these books had been considered impossible to produce,
because every picture required four plates and the square-inch cost
was rising rapidly. Hard times in the early thirties had further damp-
ened their prospects. But offset printing and new methods of color
reproduction proved to be the keys unlocking the door to a new era

30

in this genre. A wealth of new writers and artists appeared—Boris Artzybasheff, Ludwig Bemelmans, Maude and Miska Petersham, René D'Harnoncourt, Wanda Gag, and Helen and Kurt Wiese, among others. Some, like Wanda Gag, did both text and pictures for their books.

There were important new houses coming into being during the thirties. In 1935, Vernon Ives began Holiday House, Inc., the first American firm founded in this century to produce only children's books. Ives had seen the subscription books for children published in California by Helen Gentry, including *Tom Thumb*, *Rip Van Winkle*, and *The Nightingale*. He wrote to her, inviting her and her husband, David Greenhood, to come East. With them and an old friend from his Hamilton College days, Theodore Johnson, Ives founded Holiday House. "We started operations in 1935 with more optimism than capital or experience," Ives recalled later.

Illustration and text by René D'Harnoncourt in The Hole in the Wall
*(New York: Alfred A. Knopf, © 1931). Reproduced by permission of
Alfred A. Knopf, Inc.*

day, striding out across the fields
with a jug of water in her hand and
the scythe over her shoulder.

And Fritzl, where was he? He was
in the kitchen, frying a string of juicy
sausages for his breakfast. There he
sat, holding the pan over the fire,

Illustration by Wanda Gag, in Gone Is Gone *(New York: Coward &*
McCann, 1935). Reproduced by permission.

Our first office was a corner of the William E. Rudge's Sons pressroom,
and when we said we gave our books personal supervision, we meant
it. . . . Our first list was remarkable, to say the least. It consisted of two
nursery rhyme broadsides, three classic fairy tales, two of them in the
"Stocking Book" editions, my own translation of a twelfth century
book on chivalry, "Jaufry the Knight," and a realistic story of a West
African native boy, "Boomba Lives in Africa," by Caroline Singer and
Leroy Baldridge.[7]

These books were received with enthusiasm by librarians, teachers, and parents, not to mention the children themselves. A year
later, May Lamberton Becker was writing of Holiday House titles in
the *New York Herald Tribune Books:* "Books easy to the eye, stoutly
made, meant to last. They have the look of rightness a child's book
should have. Each is part of a program, part of the fulfillment of a
pledge made to itself and the public, by a publishing enterprise
trying in its own quiet way, to make its children's books notable
examples of typography and thus to train appreciation of a noble art
from an early age in the way it should go."

Nevertheless, there was difficulty with such departures from tradition as broadsides and miniature books, which bookstores were not happy to handle and libraries feared would be stolen. Many put them down as simply exotic private press productions. Sizes changed as time went on, to meet the demands of the market, but the original high quality and personalization of the initial list remained. Holiday House became the first to use silk screen for printing. Its cloth books were popular until wartime shortages curtailed them. Ives and Helen Gentry continued to do such imaginative things as sprinkling oil of cloves into the binding of *Spice on the Wind*, by Irmengarde Eberle, and binding *Lumbercamp*, by Glen Rounds, in wood. The firm also began a vogue for using miniature books as Christmas cards. Ives even wrote a book himself, the first factual volume about Russia for children to appear since the revolution. It became a part of Holiday's Lands and People series.

Three years after Holiday House began, another important firm began its career with the founding of William R. Scott, Inc., in 1938. Its children's books were unique for their experimental approach, their ability to blend the graphic and language arts, and the fact that they were based on educational theory. As a *PW* writer summarized it: "Approximate the format, imitate the style, borrow the story idea, but forget the educational theory, and the blending of all ingredients will not produce the expected result. For these are not books off an assembly line. They are custom made; designed by designers with style, line, and color that is distinctive. Distinctive as a landscape by Raoul Dufy or an abstraction by Paul Klee. Yet Scott books sell at the Macy-Gimbel price level."[8]

Scott's sense of social responsibility and his dedication to the cause of education were derived from the founder's experience with the Harriet Johnson Nursery School, a pioneer in research on children's age-level interests and language, and their psychological and physical needs. Applying what he had learned, and continued to learn, Scott produced books that charmed many parents and teachers but baffled some adult buyers of children's books who found the firm's products bearing little resemblance to those *they* had read as children. Scott editors, however, tested manuscripts on children themselves. With them, it was not a question of what experts *said* children liked, but what the child readers said *they* liked. Scott demonstrated that educational theory could be applied successfully to

33

children's books, and the firm's titles sold well over the years, significantly influencing other publishers. But it is also true that these books were often far outsold by those with no particular educational base at all.

While I may have slighted some publishers of children's books and their authors in this survey, it would be unforgivable, not to say lunatic, of me to close without mentioning what many would think was the primary event of the thirties, that is, the advent of Dr. Seuss. It may be a thrice-familiar tale, but the circumstance of his arrival should at least be recorded once more. Theodor Seuss Geisel (b. 1904) had begun his career as a commercial artist, making a reputation among other things as the originator of the familiar Flit advertisements, with the slogan that became a national byword for a time, "Quick, Henry, the Flit." Using the name Seuss, with which he had signed these ads, Geisel added "Dr." in memory of the doctorate he had studied for at Oxford, only to abandon his academic work for the art world.

He came originally to Vanguard with a set of watercolor wash drawings for a story he proposed to call *And to Think That I Saw It on Mulberry Street.* The house was so enthusiastic about his work that Marshall McClintock, the sales manager, took a dummy made up of the original drawings with him when he went on his next selling trip. Retailers proved to be just as enthusiastic, and the advance orders began to arrive; Marshall Field's, in Chicago, alone ordered 1,000 copies. In September 1937, Vanguard published the book, and by the spring of 1943, there were 31,600 copies in print.

A year later, in 1938, Vanguard published *The Five Hundred Hats of Bartholomew Cubbins,* with a first printing of 10,000. Five years later, the total in print was 19,800. Both books were heard in a radio version, and the composer Deems Taylor (1885–1966) turned out a tone poem based on *Mulberry Street.* The war years added still more to Geisel's growing reputation. It was remarkable enough that he had become, almost overnight, one of the best known writers of children's books in America, but what is truly astonishing is that he still holds that distinction nearly a half-century later.

CONCLUSION   And so the golden twenties and the somewhat less glittering thirties came to an end on a note that forecast the tremendous growth which came in the boom postwar years. Those of us who were lucky enough to have lived through those memorable early decades had the best of both worlds in our reading—the heritage of the past, and the innovations of the present. We were only somewhat distracted by radio, and the world of imagination that books created was, for me, and I assume for millions of other young Americans, an exciting world to grow up in. Publishing children's books was a relatively simple matter in those days compared with the complexities confronting publishers today, when they have to deal with television, movies, short attention spans, rapidly shifting environments, the numerous problems of education, and the intricacies of modern marketing. I don't envy them, but I wish them well, because I cling to that probably old-fashioned, and now somewhat dubious, hope that books will always be an important part of growing up enchanted, as well as informed.

NOTES

1. *Publishers Weekly,* October 16, 1926, 1592.
2. Bertha Mahoney Miller, "Children's Books in America Today," *Horn Book,* July-August 1936, 200.
3. *Publishers Weekly,* September 19, 1928, 1334.
4. *Publishers Weekly,* October 20, 1923, 1363.
5. *Publishers Weekly,* January 26, 1929, 408.
6. Edna Yost, "Who Wrote the Fifty-Cent Juveniles?" *Publishers Weekly,* May 20, 1932, 1895–98.
7. Muriel Fuller, "Vernon Ives of Holiday House," *Publishers Weekly,* April 26, 1947, 2206–8.
8. Helen K. Prager, "Story of a Unique Publishing House," *Publishers Weekly,* April 24, 1948, 1796.

———————————————*———————————————

Designing Children's Books:
A Look at the Twenties
and Thirties

BOOK DESIGNING is not a mystery, as some of its practitioners today would like to believe. Nor is it a deep creative act, despite the aspirations of a new breed called graphics communicators. Essentially, book design is a craft, a servant craft, serving author and reader. I call it so even though I am quite well aware that, in the hands of some talented individuals, this craft has been raised to the level of a minor art.

Like other craftsmen, the book designer performs a useful function. His task is to make a book readable and pleasant to hold and handle. To do his work properly, he must have respect for his materials and must know how to get the most out of his resources. These consist of not only type, paper, printing, and binding processes but also his experience and his awareness of how books were made in former times as well as in our own time. In other words, he must learn the lessons of the past. One will be a better designer if one has a broad knowledge of history and has been made sensitive aesthetically by acquaintance with the world's great art.

If the designer can make a book attractive, or even beautiful typographically, so much the better. But this is secondary and must not become an end in itself. In serving author and reader, the designer must not interject himself between them with self-conscious arrangements and clever graphic devices that interfere with communication from one to the other. As most children's books have illustrations, the typographic designer must take particular care with them to avoid introducing competitors to the pictures.

In the 1920s and 1930s, art for children's books in this country began to free itself from concepts of what was suitable held in the

37

Abe Lerner in his office at World Publishing Company, ca. 1944, soon after he left the Viking Press.

nineteenth century and the first decades of the twentieth. The revolutionary changes in painting, sculpture, and printmaking that had been taking place since the time of the Impressionists were affecting the minor arts. Under the influence of European artists, particularly from France, England, and Russia, illustration here was becoming freer, bolder, more expressive. Some of the Europeans, people like Feodor Rojankovsky (1891–1970), Roger Duvoisin (1900–1980), Kurt Wiese (1887–1974), and Boris Artzybasheff (1899–1965) emigrated to these shores and played an active role, becoming, eventually, important contributors to our modern heritage in children's books. Under the pressure of their needs, we began to develop the platemaking and printing techniques needed for reproducing their artwork more accurately and inexpensively.

The problem of the designer, who was also the production man in those days (fortunately, for the success of the final result), was to use typefaces and make layouts that accommodated the strong pictures but did not draw attention away from them. In pursuing this goal, we were given important new tools. Typefoundries brought out in the twenties and thirties an abundant array of new type designs that enabled us to work more diversely with the new, wider range of the illustrations. This was true not only of the firms producing foundry type but also of the machine-setting manufacturers, Mergenthaler Linotype and the English Monotype Corporation. Offset platemakers and printers were learning how to print halftones on antique-finish papers. Improvements in machine-made book papers enabled us to reproduce pencil and crayon drawings, and watercolors, with a higher degree of fidelity, without using the unpleasant surfaces of coated sheets. These technical advances also widened the range of techniques available to book illustrators, opening up to new generations of children a colorful richness in their books undreamed of fifty or sixty years before.

Louise Seaman's letterhead, designed by Boris Artzybasheff. Courtesy of Macmillan and Vassar College Library.

Examples of the mix of technology and typographic solutions to the problems posed by the different kinds of art can be observed in several Viking Press titles. In *Seven Simeons* by Boris Artzybasheff, the type mass works in partnership with the pictures. There is an occasional interlocking of the partners, but without detracting from the pictures. They remain, visually, the main focus of interest on all pages. The book is set in the Monotype version, cut in 1923, of John Baskerville's typeface. This particular rendering of the eighteenth-century writing master's great design has less contrast between the thick and thin strokes than the original or than the Linotype modern version. It is rather like the Intertype Baskerville. Its denser weight and somewhat staid effect act as a perfect accompanist to the Artzybasheff drawings whose line is monolithic and whose action is highly fluid.

Robert McCloskey's *Make Way for Ducklings* (1941) and Tom Robinson's *Buttons* (1938), illustrated by Peggy Bacon (b. 1895), presented the designer with exactly similar problems. Both have short texts, broadly treated lithographic drawings, and a large page size.

From Seven Simeons: A Russian Tale, *by Boris Artzybasheff (New York: The Viking Press, 1937). Book design by Milton Glick and Boris Artzybasheff. Copyright © 1937 by Boris Artzybasheff.*

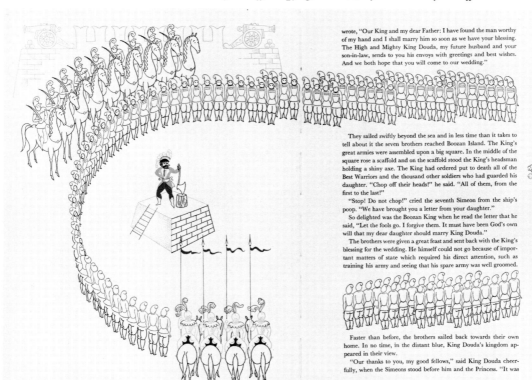

wrote, "Our King and my dear Father: I have found the man worthy of my hand and I shall marry him so soon as we have your blessing. The High and Mighty King Douda, my future husband and your son-in-law, sends to you his envoys with greetings and best wishes. And we both hope that you will come to our wedding."

They sailed swiftly beyond the sea and in less time than it takes to tell about it the seven brothers reached Boozan Island. The King's great armies were assembled upon a big square. In the middle of the square rose a scaffold and on the scaffold stood the King's headsman holding a shiny axe. The King had ordered put to death all of the Best Warriors and the thousand other soldiers who had guarded his daughter. "Chop off their heads!" he said. "All of them, from the first to the last!"

"Stop! Do not chop!" cried the seventh Simeon from the ship's poop. "We have brought you a letter from your daughter."

So delighted was the Boozan King when he read the letter that he said, "Let the fools go. I forgive them. It must have been God's own will that my dear daughter should marry King Douda."

The brothers were given a great feast and sent back with the King's blessing for the wedding. He himself could not go because of important matters of state which required his direct attention, such as training his army and seeing that his spare army was well groomed.

Faster than before, the brothers sailed back towards their own home. In no time, in the distant blue, King Douda's kingdom appeared in their view.

"Our thanks to you, my good fellows," said King Douda cheerfully, when the Simeons stood before him and the Princess. "It was

Clearly what was needed was a sturdy typeface with good color and weight, but not too bold a design. The choice was Goudy Modern. It is widely leaded in these books so as to maintain the open effect of the drawings. Goudy Modern is one of the best faces that poured out of that Niagara of type design, Frederic W. Goudy (1865–1947), creator of more than one hundred typefaces. Looking at these books today, nearly fifty years after the books were published, I must confess that I feel the choice was right.

The Three Policemen (1938) by William Pène du Bois called for an unobtrusive French touch in the typography. The Garamond type used in the book derives, in its name at least, from the great sixteenth-century French type designer to whom so many later type designers owe so much. The display lines in the chapter headings, and especially the single line of the name of the book on the title page, were set in faces called Nicholas Cochin and Le Mercure, beautiful typefaces from France which are now almost impossible to find at any shop.

From The Three Policemen: Or, Young Bottsford of Farbe Island *(New York: The Viking Press, 1938). Book design by Abe Lerner. Copyright © 1938 by William Pene Du Bois.*

The Three Policemen

or YOUNG BOTTSFORD OF FARBE ISLAND

Written and Illustrated by WILLIAM PÈNE DU BOIS

NEW YORK · THE VIKING PRESS · 1938

[Copy 2]

James Daugherty's *Andy and the Lion* presented another kind of problem. The intense action in the drawings needed space in which to be effective. It was given this space by printing the drawings on right-hand pages only, except for the few double spreads. The sparse lines of text for each picture were placed on the left-hand pages. Laid low on the page and, again, well leaded, they also lay low of the action in the pictures. The type choice here was a face called Cartoon, designed by the American Howard Trafton, and introduced into this country only the year before by a German firm, the Bauer Type Foundry. It has the look of a brush letter, and looks as though it could have been drawn with the same brush used by the artist in the making of the illustrations. The shortness of text with each picture allowed the use of all capitals, which was a necessary decision as the face has no lowercase letters. In this book they were not needed.

The diversity of technology and design presented in these five books will give some idea of how design problems were approached at the Viking Press in the 1930s.

It might prove instructive to discuss how one becomes a book designer. It is not easy to answer this question satisfactorily. There is no regular training for the job. Schools such as Cooper Union or Pratt Institute give art students only the slightest inkling. A few publishing houses may take on an apprentice. And, sometimes an artist discovers that book designing can be interesting and, in fact, deeply fulfilling. In my case, however, the scenario was quite different. Destiny (with a capital *D*) conspired with Chance (capital *C*). Together, they arranged an Amusing Incident and an Amusing Accident which brought me to this work that I love and have practiced now for more than five decades.

When the twenties began, I was eleven years old. I was an avid reader, but not from early childhood. I was born in this country, but my parents were immigrants. Their work and social life were entirely among *landsmann*, immigrants like themselves. They never read to me; books were unknown in our household except for the Hebrew prayer book which was opened only in the synagogue on holy days. But in common with most of the Jewish immigrants from Russia, my parents respected and admired reading. When they noticed me, at the age of eight or nine, bringing home books from the public library and borrowing or swapping penny dreadfuls and dime novels with my friends, they were delighted. How I came to find the world of books is vague in my memory now as I try to recall that seminal event. I think it must have been the influence of a teacher, Mr. Wolff, in one of my earliest classes at Public School No. 53 in the Bronx.

My parents didn't inquire into what I was reading. They had never heard of books like *Fanny Hill*, and *Playboy* magazine was not yet on the newstands. What did it matter to them what I read? Reading was reading. It could only be good. One read to acquire knowledge, to become educated, to learn—and learning was what immigrants worshipped.

Children's books were utterly unknown to me. My childhood reading was of Horatio Alger, Frank Meriwell, Jesse James and his brothers, the Rover Boys, and Old King Brady. These were the books that circulated among my friends. When I stumbled on the branch library in that Bronx neighborhood where we lived, I was led, I can't remember how, to Everett T. Tomlinson (1859–1931) and his stories of the American Revolution and to Joseph A. Altsheler (1862–1919), who wrote tales of the Civil War. Later came Ralph Henry Barbour (1870–1944) and his books about boys who went to prestigious preparatory schools before attending Ivy League colleges. Alas, I never made it there. The university of life was my lot, and I am still an undergraduate.

Coming into my late teens, I found more sophisticated fare, the classics and modern literature, Theodore Dreiser, Thomas Mann, Romain Rolland, not bypassing more romantic novels like *If Winter Comes* (1921), which was a raging best-seller at the time. I read the green-covered *American Mercury* magazine, published since 1924 by Knopf, and every morning I swallowed the writing of that marvelous group on the "New York World," Heywood Broun (1888–1939), Franklin P. Adams (1881–1960), Alexander Woollcott (1887–1943), and Laurence Stallings (b. 1894). I followed the doings of the Hotel Algonquin circle, which included some of those names and also George Jean Nathan (1882–1958), Harold Ross (1892–1951), John Held, Jr. (1889–1958), and, when he was in town, H. L. Mencken (1880–1956). I think I was the youngest first-night subscriber to the Theater Guild in those days. I had a seat for every play, in the first row. Never mind that it was the first row of the second balcony. As a youth of nineteen, I was leading a heady intellectual life.

This was the drive that led me to throw up a promising job at a building materials supply house where I was about to be promoted to a salesman's position, a highly coveted post in those Herbert Hoover days of building boom. It was becoming clear to me that I would be happy only by working in book publishing. I tried selling subscriptions to the newly formed Literary Guild for a few weeks, but it was boring. I asked Harold Guinzburg, owner of the Literary Guild then, if he could help me. He suggested I go to see his friend, Dick Simon, at Simon and Schuster, a fledgling three-year-old firm with a staff of fourteen where Clifton Fadiman, a young man in his twenties, was the editor. Perhaps they would have an opening. If not, he advised, I should go to the National Association of Book Publishers and register with their employment service.

With high excitement, I phoned Mr. Simon and was given an appointment that morning at eleven thirty. He listened to my story gravely and silently, slouched in his chair with his long frame stretched out to almost its full six-foot-four length. But, sorry, he told me, there was nothing available. I was crushed. I couldn't suspect that Destiny was ready to bring about the Amusing Incident mentioned earlier.

I gathered myself together and went to the National Association of Book Publishers at one o'clock the same day. Yes, they informed me, there was a job opening. Simon and Schuster was looking for an office boy. I was to apply to Leon Shimkin, office manager and head bookkeeper. Hopeful and exultant, I went there again. I was interviewed and I got the job. When Mr. Simon saw me the next day working at the office boy's desk, his eyes opened wide with surprise.

My desk was in the shipping room. My duties included opening the mail each morning, sealing and posting it at night, and operating and cleaning the mimeograph machine (no Xerox then!). How I hated cleaning that ink-filthy contraption. I also filed the duplicate invoices, and I ran errands. Errands were a routine part of the job, but when Chance played its role in that conspiracy and brought about that Amusing Accident, errands became the most exciting of my varied duties.

Like most of the Simon and Schuster employees, including Richard Simon and Leon Shimkin, our shipping clerk had come to S. and S. when it was formed, from the house of Horace Liveright. He was always familiar with what was going on at Liveright's. One day he

44

suggested I could make a little money if I would order from Liveright a copy of Eugene O'Neill's *Strange Interlude* (1928), which was to be published in a few months. He said I would get a 35 percent discount as an employee of Simon and Schuster. The retail price would be $3.50, a high figure in those days. In a year or two, he explained, I could sell the book as a first edition at a higher price, about $5.00. I figured, like a fox, that if I could make such a profit on one copy, I could make twice that amount if I ordered two, which is what I proceeded to do.

Because my working space was in the shipping room, I came to know the trucker who picked up the Simon and Schuster packages every night for delivery to stores the next day. This trucker handled the Liveright shipments also. One late afternoon he brought me a large package from Liveright. I had quite forgotten the order for *Strange Interlude* placed months before. I was puzzled and excited by this large package. What could it be?

It was not *Strange Interlude* but another Liveright book published and shipped simultaneously with the O'Neill. The label with my name on it had been attached to the wrong package. I waited for an invoice for the wrong book, but it never came. I was billed for the book I had ordered.

The wrong book was a sumptuous two-volume edition of Honoré de Balzac's *Droll Stories* (1874), illustrated in two colors by Ralph Barton. A large octavo in a slipcase, the two volumes were bound in gorgeous (to my inexperienced eyes) paper batik boards with black linen spine. I had never seen a book like that. I was overwhelmed. Until that moment, I hadn't even realized that there was more than one typeface in the world. Now the errands I had to run in my job became important. The Simon and Schuster office was on 57th Street between Fifth and Sixth Avenues. Occasionally I would take a short-cut and go through the lobby of the Heckscher Building. In a small glass case near the elevator bank in that lobby, Alfred A. Knopf, a tenant in the building, regularly displayed his new books. They too opened my eyes and caught my fancy. On my weekly wage of eighteen dollars, I began to buy Knopf books because of their handsome appearance. I learned about Nonesuch Press books and other Random House limited editions, and I started to collect them too.

I was soon led to investigating how fine books were made. I found there were such things as type specimens, paper samples, binding cloth sample books. I discovered the history of printing. I had come upon the passion of my life.

A year was spent in the office-boy job. I was promoted and became, for another year, Mr. Schuster's assistant in publicity. When an opening occurred in the production department, I moved into it. Simon and Schuster did not publish children's books then, and it was not until 1937, when I went to work for the Viking Press, that I was designing juveniles in addition to adult books. I was lucky at Viking. My boss was Milton Glick, a fine designer and production man who both taught and encouraged me. Yet he let me work on my own. And to cap it all, I had the privilege of working with May Massee (1883–1966) on many of her remarkable children's books.

Milton Glick. Photograph courtesy of Evelyn Harter Glick.

*May Massee, New York, 1928. Photograph by Alice Boughton. Reproduced
courtesy of Elizabeth Fitton Folin and Mary E. Bogan, curator,
May Massee Collection.*

May Massee's qualities as an editor of children's books are legendary. It is also well-known that she was adored by her authors and
artists. They saw that she was sympathetic to their aims and efforts.
In manner she was prim, but in her response to ideas and to quality
of writing and illustrating she was open and generous. She was tol-
erant of new work, encouraging freshness of thought and presentation if it resulted in excellence. That was the reason she used the
inventive printer's representative, William Glaser. She valued highly
his solutions to reproduction problems by which he came close to
complete fidelity in transferring artwork to the printed page.

In her personal life, May Massee was lonely. I would invite her
occasionally to dinner, sometimes to the theater. She had never been

47

to a Chinese restaurant. When I suggested it, she was willing to try it, and afterward we went several times. I remember taking her to *Pins and Needles*, the great Broadway box-office success put on the boards at first in a little, out-of-the-way theater by the International Ladies' Garment Workers Union, members of the union making up the all-amateur cast. This Harold Rome musical ran for years, undergoing several revisions to keep it fresh.

She loved it. You would not have suspected that if you dealt with her on a daily basis in the kingdom where she reigned supreme. She occupied a small room in the Viking offices on East 48th Street. In gratitude for the excellence of her contribution to the Viking list, and for the financial success of her books, Harold Guinzburg, Viking president, gave her a complete paneling of fine, light mahogany for her office walls and ceiling, with restrained fluted mahogany columns carefully placed at intervals in the walls. It was exceedingly handsome, probably what she herself had chosen. A characteristic touch in the center of the ceiling was the oval relief, carved in the mahogany, of a bull recumbent. Born in May, May Massee was a Taurus. Around the edges of the oval, the following legend was carved in the wood—in Latin. I give the English translation: "Everything in moderation, including moderation."

May Massee closely supervised every detail of her books, typography included. Although I was a newcomer to children's books when I first came to Viking, she never but once asked me to change any of my designs. She had a keen sense of what was right typographically for the texts of her books and the art they contained. We sometimes went over a detail or two, but we never discussed a philosophy of design. It was simply that we all thought alike at Viking regarding the way a book should be made. This unanimity between authors and illustrators was expressed well by Barbara Bader in her *American Picture Books from Noah's Ark to the Beast Within* (New York: Macmillan, 1976). I quote:

> If May Massee's books have one thing in common . . . they are the work of individuals—of author-illustrators with a strong personal style; and for such work, spectacular design, even distinctly original design, is counter-productive, drawing to itself attention that belongs to the word-and-picture content or, more exactly, competing with it for attention. The men at Viking were not designers of this sort; unless one fixes on it, one notices not the make-up but the book. (p. 198)

Helen Gentry printing on her Colt Press, at 605 Commercial Street, San Francisco, early 1930s. Photograph by Peter Stackpole. Reproduced by permission. Courtesy of Evelyn Harter Glick.

It is fair to say that this attitude was typical of the better known houses in those days. It was not confined to Viking. Arthur W. Rushmore (1883–1955) of Harper's and Helen Gentry of Holiday House were among the sound and sensitive designers of children's books, and there were others.

We can look back on the twenties and thirties as the time when this awakening of design and reproduction possibilities came about. And with that backward glance, we honor those spirits in the writing, illustrating, and editing of children's books who have taken us and our child audiences into a higher realm of accomplishment with man's greatest invention, The Book.

Printer's mark, dated 1927, for Arthur Rushmore's Golden Hind Press, Madison, New Jersey. Reproduced by permission of Mrs. Delight Lewis.

ANNE MACLEOD

———————————*———————————

Literary and Social Aspects of Children's Books of the Twenties and Thirties

By AMERICAN STANDARDS, the period from 1920 to 1940 is a long stretch of social history. It began less than two years before the end of the First World War, the war that marked the close of an era in Western culture. When the period ended, the country was within two years of entering the Second World War, already rolling across Europe and the Far East. In the twenty years bracketed by these catastrophic events, the United States went from a hectic prosperity to the depths of a prolonged depression, which lifted only as the country mobilized for war. In other words, these two decades were a period of vivid social change, in a country in which social change has been the norm rather than the exception.

Children's books of the twenties and thirties took the impress of the cultural changes around them. It would certainly not be possible to construct an accurate record of the social, political, or economic developments of this nation between 1920 and 1940 from the evidence in children's stories—that one cannot do in any period. Yet the shifts in cultural attitudes are there, recorded in the indirect way in which children's attitudes always document the time, and expressed in the values the books held out to young readers. It is possible to trace lingering ties with pre-World War I society as these stretched ever more thinly through the twenties, until they virtually disappeared in the changed world of the Great Depression. And it is possible, too, to see how books of the thirties embodied and confirmed an idea of childhood that would dominate children's literature for the next thirty-five years, a fusion of realism and idealization of childhood and American family life which has altered fundamentally only in the past fifteen to twenty years.

I will consider here the family story, the mainstream domestic fiction of children's literature, whose setting is contemporary with the period in which it was written. Family stories tend to express most plainly the attitudes we want to understand: the concepts of childhood and of family life, the values adults hoped to pass along to children, and the overall view of life and circumstance that framed the stories. Generally speaking, children's books change with the slower and deeper currents of their time, rather than as the surface of culture changes. There was little of the flashing glitter of the Roaring Twenties in that decade's children's stories; the literature was still deeply rooted in an earlier era. Though the settings and events were contemporary, many of the basic attitudes and most of the social concepts in 1920s children's books were much like those in turn-of-the-century fiction, and in some respects like those of the post-Civil War period. Which is to say that the basic view of character and society was sentimental, and the recurrent themes were of striving and achieving in a mobile, competitive society. Twenties children's fiction still dealt in simple moralities and in sentimental solutions to unsentimental problems. Strokes of luck and unsolicited benevolence solved problems of poverty, injustice, and class disadvantage.

Certainly the idealized children of twenties books owed a great deal to their turn-of-the-century counterparts. Romanticized children were still popular. They turned up like emissaries from a better world to improve the lives of joyless adults, exactly as they had a generation before. Laura Richards (1850–1943) wrote a sequel to *Captain January* (1890), that highly romanticized story of a foundling child, and *Star Bright* (1927) was still, like its predecessor, a perfect example of late nineteenth-century idealization of childhood. Like Anne of Green Gables and Rebecca of Sunnybrook Farm, *Star Bright* has all the attributes of a romantic child: she is imaginative, affectionate, responsive to beauty, especially nature's beauties, and of a dramatic, literary turn of mind. Even as she approaches womanhood, she retains a childlike impetuosity and egocentricity. Indeed, this child-woman expresses her deepest feelings in obscure Shakespearean quotations—which gives her conversation a very odd flavor—and is generally about twice as fey as Anne or Rebecca, but fundamentally, her character and her role in the lives of others are much like theirs.

Boys were idealized, too, but their qualities were different because their destinies were tied firmly to the outer world. Where girls were encouraged to brighten the lives of those immediately around them and to preserve the charms of childhood as long as possible, boys had a larger sphere to grow into. A boy's character and actions always pointed toward adult life, and fiction frequently allowed a boy to take a hand in adult affairs. *St. David Walks Again* is exemplary. This 1928 novel by Christine Jope-Slade is both a portrait of an idealized boy and a round of applause for American enterprise. Though less gracefully written, it offers in some ways an interesting parallel to *Little Lord Fauntleroy* (New York: Scribner; London: Warne, 1886), published nearly two generations earlier.

The story concerns two American children, David and Felicity, who go to Cornwall to live with their grandfather after the death of their parents. The children's situation is complicated by estrangement, just as Little Lord Fauntleroy's was; their English grandfather of ancient family never forgave his son for marrying an American, and he is also convinced that David, when he inherits the family seat, Hoblyn House, will probably turn it into a hotel. David, at age twelve, is described as "a very manly little boy. No fiddle-faddle about David. He looked like a man, . . . his chin had a man-jut, and his shoulders were man-set."

The children find Hoblyn House and the fishing village around it asleep, like the castle in Sleeping Beauty. Grandfather hates the twentieth century and lives as much as possible as though it were two hundred years earlier, using candlelight, wearing eighteenth-century clothing, and so on. The economy of the village is paralyzed: the fish no longer come, and no one has the energy or enterprise to do anything new. The people look for miracles or an authority to initiate changes. Such passivity is anathema to David: "He was a bold fellow . . . the history of the Hoblyns and the pluck of American pioneers had gone to the making of David. . . . From his American mother he inherited new, gay, courageous ways of looking at old problems, fresh ways of solving them."[1]

Still, when David solves the problems of Hoblyn House (as, of course, he does), his methods have little in them that is new, fresh, or twentieth-century. For all he cries out against his grandfather's rejection of the present—"It is wicked! . . . yesterday is yesterday . . . you can't have it over again"—he restores local prosperity by reviving the villagers' belief in the ghost of St. David, who brings luck to fishermen. And though he says, "there aren't any miracles . . . unless PEOPLE did them," the fish miraculously return on their own and the economy revives without the introduction of any new industry.[2] Like Grandfather, the author seems to want the past retrieved more or less intact.

Nevertheless, muddled message and all, *St. David* is interesting for its attempt to weigh the merits of the Old World against those of the New, and for its conclusion that history and noble tradition are worthless without New World pluck and enterprise. The theme was a favorite in children's books of the post-Civil War era and had not yet, in the twenties, lost its appeal. Even with its aristocratic ruffles and flourishes, *St. David Walks Again* is recognizable as one more celebration of American "get up and git."

The point of most American enterprise was, of course, to get ahead, to "rise in the world," as Horatio Alger always put it. And just behind the eager wish to get ahead was a general preoccupation with class and wealth, pervasive in post-Civil War society, and still highly visible in children's books of the twenties. If Alger's wooden simplicities seemed out of date after World War I, Frances Hodgson Burnett curiously combined admiration for both democratic character and aristocratic privilege. That this was a common American attitude, the *St. David* story attests.

The most popular nineteenth-century model, however, seems to have been Margaret Sidney's *Five Little Peppers* series, usually with mother left out. Sidney (1844–1924) described poor but worthy children, "naturally genteel," who were adopted or befriended by affluent gentlefolk, a story that was a favorite in the twenties. Such a plot offered useful scope to the author, who could first show children bravely struggling with hardship and then deliver them to a better life, with money, protection, and education. It was also wonderfully revealing of an author's attitudes toward poverty, character, class, and material wealth.

In the twenties, convention insisted that poverty carried no stigma, but at the same time, improvement of one's lot was all but mandatory for an American. To be born in a log cabin was an asset to many a career, but to rise above such humble beginnings was the real point. The climb from a lower to a higher economic level, however, involved more than simple finances in the American credo.

54

Class and culture had to be considered. Authors of mainstream children's books endorsed the genteel tradition that linked wealth with cultivation—it would never do to bestow real affluence on a lower class child who had neither manners nor finer feelings, who felt no responses to beauty and art, or who worse yet, was vicious and depraved.

Yet the lower classes obviously bred some such offspring, who posed some thorny questions. Were they entirely redeemable by a change of environment? If so, then were class differences wholly the product of circumstance—the luck of the draw? And, if not, then wasn't the social mobility that was at the heart of the American dream a threat to the genteel class—already faced with waves of Silas Lamphams, rich but hopelessly vulgar. These were vexing questions for authors who were not, after all, social philosophers, and the plot devices they chose to handle the awkwardness were usually clumsy. The particular machinery varied, but the basic solution to the problem always involved the notion of inborn quality—a "natural" gentility, which qualified certain children to move gracefully into a higher class.

This, too, was an old idea. Most nineteenth-century "rags to riches" stories leaned on the concept of inborn character to make class shifts palatable to the middle classes. Even Alger's heroes, whose rise on the social scale was modest rather than spectacular, were always distinguished from their non-rising street fellows by unusual decency and manners, characteristics sometimes attributed to genteel forebears who had fallen into poverty but who still beqeathed good character to their progeny.

Whatever the source, sterling inner character had to be there if a child was to make the move from a lower to a higher class. Fortunately, those in a position to help were always able to spot the sterling beneath the dross. *John and Susanne* is the story of an orphaned brother and sister adopted by an outstandingly genteel family. When the children run away from a ghastly asylum in New York, fate delivers them to the well-to-do Fairleys, who live an affluent and admirably cultivated life in the Connecticut countryside. The Fairleys already have three ideal children, but they add the waifs to their menage without missing a beat. John, at five, is bursting with artistic talent, which is immediately recognized by father, fortuitously an artist himself. More important, both children brim with inner

55

Kicking and struggling, he swung himself out

JOHN AND SUSANNE

BY
EDITH BALLINGER PRICE
Author of "GARTH: ABLE SEAMAN," "THE HAPPY VENTURE,"
"THE FORTUNE OF THE INDIES," "BLUE MAGIC," etc.

ILLUSTRATED BY
THE AUTHOR

THE CENTURY CO.
New York   &   London

John and Susanne, *by Edith Ballinger Price (New York and London: The Century Co., 1926). Copyright, 1926, by The Century Co. Courtesy of E. P. Dutton.*

character, as mother easily discerns: she "looked very straight into their eyes [and] found something very good back there."[3] There are reliable signals of their worthiness throughout: Susanne responds to natural beauty, finding religious meaning in the glories of nature, while John's artistic genius and straightforward honesty more than justify his adoption. As a girl, Susanne is never suspected of any particular genius but she makes a place for herself by gratitude, a feeling for beauty, and—not least—practical usefulness. Both children work very hard at improving their grammar.

As the family absorbs the orphans into its daily life, a reader gets a detailed picture of ideal family activities. There are art lessons for John, home dramatics and reading aloud, toys, space, and a riding horse freely shared. Most important, the parents always have time to be with the children.

Lest the reader mistake all this for an inevitable consequence of wealth, the author supplies an episode that throws clear light on the value system which distinguishes gentility from mere affluence. A "fashionable" family comes to visit, bringing their "over-fed and over-dressed" children. Both parents and children are snobbish; they scorn John and Susanne, openly wondering at the place they are given in the Fairley family. Though the adopted waifs feel the slights, Susanne returns good for evil in the best moral tradition when she saves over-fed Myrtle from a runaway horse. Once the visitors leave, Mrs. Fairley draws the lesson for Susanne, telling her that "ladies" are defined, not by wealth, but by "the way they feel inside."[4] Genteel sensibility was very much alive in twenties fiction, even if it dwelt side by side with a crasser taste for material well-being.

The value system of most authors included the doctrine of hard work alongside the comfort of affluence, and many a fictional child worked first and found comfort afterward. In yet another orphan story, a sister and brother struggle for months to avoid the poor farm, picking apples, fishing for lobster, growing their own food when they can. It is a heroic effort, but without real hope of success, since, even if they manage to live, they cannot possibly also go to school and "amount to something," as the older sister recognizes. In time, of course, a responsible adult steps in to restore their fortunes and take on the role of guardian until they come of age. Yet the experience of hard work has had its value, as Betsey reflects when it is all over: ". . . the hardship, the struggle fused into a shining steel bar which somehow ran through her and made her strong."[5]

Clearly, the twenties were a period of transition in American attitudes toward the benefits of learning to work, on the one hand, and a child's right to a protected, carefree childhood, on the other. In a 1927 novel, an adult remarks, "I don't believe it hurts a boy to work a little," adding, "but I'd hate to see a boy work so hard that he didn't have a good time."[6]

The effort to encompass both value systems without resort to orphans is apparent in *Dan's Boy*, a novel with a mild debt to *Captains Courageous* (1897) and a strong message about how a boy should be brought up. Alden, the central character, is a cosseted seven-year-old, the son of affluent, over-protective parents. A series of unlikely events brings him to the forest cabin of old Dan, an odd-job man and one of Nature's noblemen. For several months, Dan believes that

"THEY THOUGHT MAYBE YOU'D RATHER BE ALONE"
(Page 77)

DAVID IVES
A STORY OF ST. TIMOTHY'S

BY
ARTHUR STANWOOD PIER

WITH ILLUSTRATIONS BY
FRANKLIN WOOD

BOSTON AND NEW YORK
HOUGHTON MIFFLIN COMPANY
The Riverside Press Cambridge
1922

David Ives: A Story of St. Timothy's, by Arthur Stanwood Pier and illustrated by Franklin Wood (Boston and New York: Houghton Mifflin Co., 1922). Copyright, 1921, by Perry Mason Company. Copyright, 1922, by Arthur Stanwood Pier.

Alden is his own son (explaining this plot is out of the question) and treats him accordingly—which means that he kindly, but firmly, instills his own values in the boy. And so Alden learns to work, both at home, as part of the household, and away, to earn money. He also learns cleanliness, self-discipline, competitiveness, and getting along with other boys, which includes fighting when necessary. This education gives him the pride he must have to succeed in a competitive society: "Pride that makes us lift our chins and work a little more is the pride that wins the prize." By the time he returns to his real home, "tough and tanned and freckled," Alden is fit to resume a life of privilege without being spoiled by it.[7]

The values this book promotes—a healthy toughness of body, the will to compete, self-discipline, and a measure of both humility and manly stoicism—were all staples in books for and about boys in the twenties. And as the educational benefits of hard work or hard knocks were less and less relevant to a middle class childhood, the job of passing these values along to boys became more and more the responsibility of schools. School stories aimed at an affluent middle class multiplied. Arthur Pier (1874–1966) wrote ten prep school novels, published between 1919 and 1931, that make sport of this vehicle for teaching manly character to boys, particularly to those boys whose homes were wealthy but short on gentility. Quite typically, a teacher in one of Pier's novels deplores the "influences prevailing in the homes of some of our excessively solvent citizens."[8] Obviously, the schools—all private in Pier's novels—were to provide the civilizing influences such homes did not.

Ideals for girls were neither identical with those for boys nor as unambiguous. A girl might or might not be encouraged to develop a strong, healthy body. By the end of the decade, she might be urged to be competitive in a girl's sport or in a feminine pursuit like canning or quilting contests at a state fair. Assuredly, she would not be encouraged to compete with boys, and tomboys who did always had to learn more acceptable ways of using their energy. Work might or might not be an important part of a girl's upbringing; if it was, it was usually work close to home.

But of all the ambiguities in attitudes toward girls, the greatest surrounded authors' feelings about feminine independence. Young girls in twenties fiction were quite often spirited creatures. Some were practical and enterprising, like the various orphans who fended for themselves and their younger brothers or sisters until help arrived. Some were sturdy tomboys, determined to do anything a boy could do and usually successful at it. Some were free spirits like Rebecca of Sunnybrook Farm: they dared things and assumed leadership because they had more imagination than anyone else around.

But while a boy's path ran more or less straight from boyhood to manhood, with the strengths of one phase of life also appropriate to the next, the same was not true for girls. Every story that took a girl into adolescence recognized that convention required a young woman to accept more restrictions on her life than did a preadolescent girl and that independence of mind was at best an uncomfortable trait in a woman. Whether or not the authors agreed with these conventions, their books did not set out to break them. Adolescent heroines ultimately accepted—without rebellion—their secondary roles, no matter how triumphantly independent they had been as children. Only the authors' enthusiasm for a prolonged childhood for girls (but not for boys) suggests their regret for the metamorphosis their heroines were compelled to undergo; the transition itself was usually fogged over by a cloud of romance.

A 1924 novel titled *A Girl of the Plains Country* is typical. An orphaned girl is raised by her guardian, the manager of the ranch she is to inherit, with the idea that she will take over when she comes of age. As a young girl, she is active, sometimes daring, occasionally outspoken. When she reaches her mid-teens, still "slim and undeveloped," adults take to warning her against early marriage and the reader begins to expect that she will in fact become ranch manager in her own right. By the end of the book, however, the direction has shifted completely. At a mere seventeen, this heroine finds her romantic mate, and it is clear that she will marry—early—and never manage the ranch on her own, after all. It is a characteristically mixed message. Authors often showed young girls fully capable of both the spirit and the physical skills routinely attributed to boys, but they drew back at the implications of such equality for adult life. On this subject, as on others, books of the twenties reflected a compromise between change and tradition.

Over time, the success theme diminished in this fiction, or at least moved closer to homely reality. From adoptions by well-to-do gentry or discoveries of long-lost mortgages, authors turned more often to blue ribbons at the fair and the first prize in the school race. Yet dreams of striving and winning, of prizes and a shining future, continued to rule—until circumstance changed the rules.

The calamitous end to the twenties boom and the swift decline into devastating depression affected every part of American culture, including mainstream children's literature. Changes came unevenly, of course, but overall there is no mistaking the difference the thirties made in the world reflected in children's books. It became in many respects a more realistic world. Romanticism faded, and the sentimentality that had clung to 1920s fiction all but disappeared. There was a new crop of writers who looked at their society differently. They idealized some of what they saw, certainly, but they saw differently, aspired to different things, and abandoned once and for all the plainly sentimental literary conventions of the nineteenth century.

Essentially, thirties writers shifted the focus of children's fiction.

Where authors of the twenties tended to look toward the future, putting achievement, social mobility, and material affluence at the center of their stories, thirties authors turned their attention from future to present, and from status within society to relationships within families. The characteristic children's book of the thirties was the family story, in which relations between children and parents, children and children, and children and community constituted the plot, while childhood itself furnished the major theme.[9] Even the time span of the stories contracted. Where stories of the twenties often took their young protagonists within sight of adult life, thirties fiction was more likely to stay firmly within childhood, focusing on a single year, a few months, or one summer. Plots were episodic and small-gauged as authors tried to re-create the experiences and the feelings of childhood.

To a remarkable degree, the various works of fiction shared a common outlook. Taken together, the work of such prominent authors of the period as Eleanor Estes (b. 1906), Elizabeth Enright (1909–1968), Doris Gates (b. 1901), Rachel Field (1894–1942), and Elizabeth Coatsworth (b. 1893) created a coherent concept of children, family, and childhood that shaped the family story for decades. If that concept was mildly idealized (and it surely was), it was an ideal widely shared in middle class America. If family life was not always just like the fictional model (and doubtless it was not), most Americans would have agreed that it should have been.

The ideal began and ended with security, love, and protection for the young. Children were integral parts of their families, yet a child lived at a little distance from the serious concerns of adult life. Middle class American culture had reached a consensus about childhood, seeing it as a time for growing and learning under adult protection, a time, above all, for innocent happiness—a season in the sun before the shadow of adult responsibility fell.

Patterns of family life in fiction reflected the consensus. Children and adults lived together within a system of mutual affection and responsibility, with the weight of responsibility solidly on the adult side. A child's part was to be affectionate, cooperative, and responsive to adult guidance. Love between parent and child was fundamental to the concept of family life portrayed in these books, so children must be lovable—and so they were. Fictional children were amiable and good-hearted and childlike; they neither aped nor challenged adults. Though they took responsibility appropriate to their age, it was for adults to make the serious decisions, to nurture and direct children, and—most important—to provide the security on which childhood depended absolutely.

The clear line between adult and child roles, however, neither separated the generations nor made for authoritarian rule at home. On the contrary: in children's fiction, relations between child and adult were almost always warm and easy. Children had ready access to their parents, and parents were sensitive and responsive to children's needs. Adults, in fact, sometimes crossed over from their own sphere into a child's, joining in children's activities and pleasures. In Coatsworth's *Alice-All-by-Herself*, Alice and her mother and father create a special room in the attic for rainy days. Here is the scene when they first use it:

> Alice's father and mother were already there, popping corn over the stove and pouring it into a yellow kitchen bowl, with a big pat of butter on a dish and a salt cellar beside it. There was a giant basket of apples, too, and a sweet-smelling bouquet of herbs and the candles lighted. You could hear the rain falling so lightly and steadily on the roof, and the whisper and furling of the flames and the gay dancing and popping of the corn. There was a little chair waiting ... beside the row of old bound St. Nicholases. ...."[10]

The whole thirties image of an ideal home and family is in that passage.

The adult domain, on the other hand, was not a child's territory, particularly in time of trouble, though children were sometimes aware of family problems. In Enright's *Thimble Summer*, nine-year-old Garnet understands that the drought worries her farmer father: "Tonight her father would sit late in the kitchen, worried and silent, doing sums on a piece of paper. Long after everyone else had gone to bed, the lamp would burn and he would be there by himself."[11] But Garnet is never drawn into her father's troubles, nor is she asked to share his fears; such matters belonged to the grown-up world.

I don't want to give the impression that hard reality was consistently filtered out of children's literature in this period, for that is not the case. I have said that thirties fiction was more realistic than that of the preceding decade, and it was. The fairy tale plots in which fictional characters moved from misery to bliss by way of sudden luck had given way to stories much closer to the experience of ordinary people.

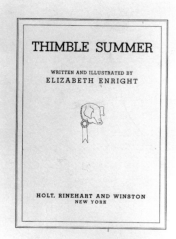

THIMBLE SUMMER

WRITTEN AND ILLUSTRATED BY
ELIZABETH ENRIGHT

HOLT, RINEHART AND WINSTON
NEW YORK

"We're all right, Papa," said Citronella. "But we're awfully hungry."

"I'll go telephone the folks at home," volunteered Mr. Freebody. "So's they won't have to worry no longer. You better take the little girls down to the lunch wagon for a bite. Only place that's open at this hour."

The lunch wagon was down by the railroad tracks; neither Garnet nor Citronella had ever been there before. It was full of bright yellow light, and cigar smoke, and powerful food smells. It was wonderful to go there so late at night and eat fried egg sandwiches and apple pie and tell everybody what had happened to them.

"Yes sir!" said Mr. Freebody coming in the door. "Don't you be fooled! Those ain't two little girls you see settin' up there; those are two genuwine bookworms, couldn't stop reading long enough to come home. Planning to take up permanent residence in the liberry from now on, ain'tcha?"

Everyone laughed.

"Just the same," whispered Garnet to Citronella. "I sort of wish they hadn't found us until morning. Then we could have told our grandchildren that once we stayed in the public library all night long!"

Chapter VI

JOURNEY

THE LONG days of August were filled with activity. The barn took shape rapidly and it was going to be a fine one. Every now and then Mr. Freebody would pause before it and shake his head.

"My, that sure is a pretty barn," he would say dreamily. "That sure is pretty as a peach."

The warm air rang with the sound of saw and hammer. While the men worked on the barn Garnet and her mother had their hands full with the house and garden; for now the garden was yielding in all its abundance. It was hard to keep up with it. When you had finished picking all the beans it was time to pick the yellow squashes, shaped like hunting horns. And when you got through with the squash it was time for the beans again. And then you had to hurry, hurry and gather the bursting ripe tomatoes from the heavy vines, for canning. Then there were beets and carrots to be attended to; and after that it was time for the beans again.

"Beans never know when to stop!" said Garnet's mother in annoyance.

Thimble Summer, *by Elizabeth Enright (New York: Holt, Rinehart and Winston, 1938).*

But the thirties view of children, both as protagonists and audience, kept literary realism within bounds, with the line of demarcation falling, usually, between people and circumstance. Writers were wiling to tell children that life was not always perfect, but, generally, they chose to identify trouble with impersonal forces, like nature or economics. Personal malevolence, violence, hatred, and despair had little place in their concept of what was appropriate for children.

As one might expect, the commonest misfortune in the stories was poverty, but it was not a very grinding form of poverty the fiction described. It caused neither bitterness nor severe deprivation, and it rarely set the poorer children apart in any important way from those who were better off. Only the migrant workers of *Blue Willow* were painfully poor, and even here, Gates avoided acknowledging the worst social consequences of real poverty. Estes's Moffat family stories were more typical: though the Moffats were poor enough to receive some haphazard charity from their neighbors, it made no difference socially. The Moffats' rented house backed up to the garden of Janey's best friend, whose family was well off enough to enjoy polished floors, thick rugs, and luncheons served by a maid. Yet the

THE
MOFFATS

by ELEANOR ESTES

ILLUSTRATED BY LOUIS SLOBODKIN

HARCOURT, BRACE AND COMPANY
NEW YORK

BLUE WILLOW

BY DORIS GATES

ILLUSTRATED BY PAUL LANTZ

THE VIKING PRESS · NEW YORK · 1940

Blue Willow *by Doris Gates, illustrated by Paul Lantz (New York: The Viking Press, 1940). Copyright © 1940 by Doris Gates.*

sizable economic gap put no social distance between the two little girls, nor was there any difference in the families' standards, values, or manners. The Moffats' poverty was accidental and superficial; it neither characterized them nor drove a class wedge between them and their neighbors. Thirties fiction had moved away from the edgy class consciousness of the twenties.

On the whole, the outer world as pictured in children's fiction was benign. Stories encouraged children to move outward and become acquainted with their communities; indeed, a child's exploration of the world beyond home made up the plot of many a thirties book. That children must establish a connection with the larger society was fundamental to the philosophy that shaped the literature, as one author of the period explained: "A fully rounded life," she wrote in 1935, "must not be egocentric, but must be centered in the society of which that individual is a part."[12] It was important to a child's growing up to know and trust the community and its people, and to learn to look beyond superficial differences to the common humanity that lay beneath. The messages in thirties fiction on the subject were consistently upbeat: the outside world held some hazards, to be sure, but on balance, the good very much outweighed the bad. Children need not fear the world. "Little girl," says Janey Moffat's police chief, "don't be afraid of a policeman . . . or of anything. . . . Remember this. A policeman is for your protection."[13]

In its own way, then, children's literature recorded and responded to cultural change over two momentous decades. Some of the new directions of the thirties can be attributed to new authors, who were often more sophisticated writers than their twenties predecessors, who had both a more coherent, less stereotyped vision to convey and better developed literary skills with which to express it. But the changes in children's fiction, and the particular directions taken, also recorded real shifts in the American outlook over twenty changing years. When we look at them now, some seem no more than logical. The twenties' preoccupation with striving and achieving was obviously out of step with an economy in severe decline. In the face of an economic collapse of the magnitude of the Great Depression, it is not surprising that fiction for the young turned away from dreams of material gain and upward mobility to center on the plainer comforts of home and family. For Americans, home had always been a haven from the rigors of a competitive society; now it was a shelter from the cold winds of economic fear and future uncertainty. If the social order was manifestly insecure, then security must be located in family and community; if everything else was in flux, if the future was clouded, then home must be where the stream ran clear and steady, with no fearful undercurrents.

What is surprising, though, I think, is the calm serenity of the thirties stories, the faith in human nature that pervaded them all, the optimism that survived a massive fracture of the social system. A literature that might well have been anxious or bitter or despairing was none of these, not at all at any level. The stream ran clear and steady, with no fearful undercurrents.

This fictional picture should not be dismissed as pure myth manufactured for children, or as a peculiar unworldliness on the part of the authors. There is truth as well as wish in these stories. Families of the thirties could and did function as the stories said—closely integrated, yet psychologically separated along generational lines. For all that times were hard and families strained to meet daily needs, children did grow up at some protective remove from adult concerns; they knew and didn't know, at the same time. Russell Baker's memoir of his thirties childhood says it well: "The occasional outbursts of passion that flickered across my childhood were like summer storms. The sky clouded suddenly, thunder rumbled, lightning flashed, and I trembled a few moments, then just as swiftly the sky turned blue again and I was basking contentedly in the peace of innocence."

Baker also confirms that the temperate mood of the stories had its counterpart in reality. Listening to adults talk night after night around the kitchen table, he was, he writes, "receiving an education in the world and how to think about it. What I absorbed most deeply was not information but attitudes, ways of looking at the world that were to stay with me for many years. Sometimes their talk about the Depression was shaded with anger, but its dominant tones were good humor and civility. The anger was never edged with bitterness or self-pity."[14]

So the children's books told the truth, as they always do. It was not the whole truth; it never is, in this, or perhaps in any literature, but it is the kind of truth difficult to extract from more objectively complete histories. Whatever surface messages children's books send out, they also transmit the emotional tone of their culture.

67

Twenties books conveyed the nervous energy of a society whose hopes were for success and achievement in the material world, whereas thirties fiction reflected a society hunkered down to wait out hard times, returning for reassurance to family and community, taking what comfort it could in human warmth, and enduring, on the whole, with tolerance and good humor.

In retrospect, I suppose one could ask—someone usually does—whether these books were "good for children." In a society that went from boom to bust, from a heedless postwar gala to a second world war, were authors justified in telling children that people were basically good, that society was essentially decent, and that children could grow up to find a place in a rational world? Were children steadied by their season in the sun, and armed against the sea of troubles that awaited them? Or were they crippled by their innocence and paralyzed by an inability to recognize evil before it overwhelmed them?

Obviously, the answers to such questions involve the most basic convictions about the meaning and purpose of childhood. It is just these convictions that change with changing times, and that determine how adults construct and conduct childhood for children, and, most certainly, how they write for children. I do not mean to offer answers here—only the observation that today's literature for children says more plainly than anything else that American attitudes toward childhood, society, the world, and the future have moved miles and miles and years and years away from the 1920s and 1930s—but that is a whole other story.

NOTES

1. Christine Jope-Slade, *St. David Walks Again* (New York: Harper & Bros., 1928), pp. 25, 26.
2. Ibid., pp. 59, 62.
3. Edith Ballinger Price, *John and Susanne* (New York: The Century Co., 1926), p. 60.
4. Ibid., p. 133.
5. Mabel L. Robinson, *All by Ourselves* (New York: Dutton, 1924), p. 253.
6. Margaret Ashmun, *Mother's Away* (New York: Macmillan, 1927), p. 166.
7. Bertha Cobb and Ernest Cobb, *Dan's Boy* (Newton Upper Falls, Mass.: ARLO, 1926), pp. 156, 168.

8. Arthur Pier, *David Ives* (Boston: Houghton Mifflin, 1922), p. 28.
9. This was as true of the many thirties stories set in other countries or other periods as it was of contemporary stories with American settings.
10. Elizabeth Coatsworth, *Alice-All-by-Herself* (New York: Macmillan, 1937), p.74.
11. Elizabeth Enright, *Thimble Summer* (New York: Holt, Rinehart and Winston, 1938), p. 7.
12. Margaret T. Raymond, "Bread for Adolescence," *Horn Book* 11 (September 1935):302.
13. Eleanor Estes, *The Moffats* (New York: Harcourt, Brace and World, 1941), p. 51.
14. Russell Baker, *Growing Up* (New York: Congden & Weed, 1982), pp. 42, 117.

Children's Reading Room of the Cleveland Public Library, 1920s.
Courtesy of the Cleveland Public Library.

———————————✳———————————

The Leadership Network in Children's Librarianship: A Remembrance

WHEN ONE LOOKS at library leaders of the 1920s and 1930s, it is clear that there are some whose personalities and abilities would have drawn significant attention and who would no doubt have been leaders in almost any field they had chosen. There were also, however, several factors in the development of the library profession during the first quarter of this century, specifically public library services to youth, which contributed to the potential for growth of leadership. Three factors had an especially strong effect.

First there was the attitude of librarians of public libraries toward children and their access to libraries. From the beginning of her career as librarian at Hartford Public Library in the 1880s, Caroline Hewins urged that children be encouraged to visit the library and that books of interest to them be made available. Before 1900, at American Library Association (ALA) conferences, prominent librarians had first proposed opening libraries to children, and before the turn of the century several large public libraries had begun providing service to children. Though variable and limited, a beginning had been made. As library administrators permitted services to children, they had to appoint assistants to take care of the new users. As such services were extended to the branches, more assistants were needed. As more children's librarians were added, an administrator to head children's services became essential in larger city library systems. These supervisory positions offered opportunities for leadership development.

The second factor was the early availability of specialized training for children's librarianship. Establishment of the special course for children's librarians at Pratt Institute Library School in Brooklyn in 1898 and the opening in Pittsburgh of the Training School for Children's Librarians in 1900 provided the means for obtaining such specialized professional training. To each school came young women from across the country. Those who graduated or received certificates soon found positions in the new public library children's departments. The opportunities for leadership were many in these early days, and most of the leaders of the 1920s and 1930s mentioned in this paper came from these two schools.

The third factor was the organization in 1900 of the ALA Section for Library Work with Children. At least nine librarians who worked with children attended the ALA conference that year and proposed the section's establishment. Since then, children's librarians have had a meeting at ALA every year. At changing conference sites across the country there were opportunities to share experiences with new children's librarians and maintain contacts already made. The librarians serving children felt a part of the library profession. Their experiences as officers of the section brought their leadership skills to the attention of their colleagues and of chief librarians. Such roles were often preludes to recognition and to continuing leadership at local, state, and national levels.

For children's librarians in public libraries, these three conditions facilitating leadership development were in place early in the twentieth century. By the twenties and thirties, there were active leaders involved in public library children's services who made further advances. Their programs were generally carried out and their goals attained.

The situation in the early history of school libraries, however, was not as favorable for the development of leadership. Mary Hall was promoting school libraries by 1906. She was active in the National Education Association (NEA) Library Department, which, however, was discontinued in 1924. In 1913 she helped organize the Library Section of the National Council of Teachers of English. In 1914 she was involved in organizing the ALA School Libraries Section. When it was approved in 1915, she served as its first president. Rather than school librarians, it was teachers-college librarians who joined Hall to petition for the ALA School Libraries Section. Efforts were dissipated and progress was slow. The need for school library service development, however, was clearly evident.

English teachers needed school libraries to teach effectively. Yet many school libraries were staffed by teacher-librarians selected from present faculty, usually from the English department, or trained in teachers colleges, even up through the 1930s. School administrators normally hired new staff members from teachers colleges, and they went to them for school library personnel as well. Some of the teachers-college training courses were very good, but students had little or no contact with the library profession. School boards did not recognize libraries within the school as essential. School administrators, usually trained in teachers colleges and schools of education themselves, had seldom been introduced in their training to school libraries as a fundamental resource. Money was inadequate to provide space, personnel, or good curricula, and school libraries were not on the priority list. When libraries were provided they were most often staffed by a clerk or assistant at a salary level below that of teacher if not by teacher-librarians.

The pattern was broken in California. The California School Library Association, organized in 1915, proposed, lobbied for, and in 1917 saw signed into law, authorization of a school librarian's certificate, recognizing library school-trained librarians as professionals, whose salaries should be comparable to teachers' salaries. Trained school librarians were added to faculties in California schools, and at good salaries. With more school librarians, improved school libraries, and the active state association, library leaders appeared in various parts of California earlier than in other parts of the country.

To this general situation there were, of course, individual exceptions. For example, in Detroit a school library department was begun in 1922 and it included elementary and junior high as well as high schools. In Newark, New Jersey, a supervisor of school libraries and audiovisual services was appointed in 1929.

By the 1920s, state school library supervisors trained in library schools were beginning to influence the quality of school library personnel, book collections, and facilities in Minnesota, New York, and Michigan. In the 1930s, the state school library supervisors in several southern states expanded this key group of leaders. State supervisors were especially important since the basic authority for public schools was in the state. During the thirties, many demonstration or practice schools in teacher training institutions added library school-trained school librarians and demonstrated very good library service. Teachers and administrators in training could actually see and come to appreciate their value.

Divided loyalties between the NEA and ALA for professional affiliation created problems. In some school systems membership in NEA was made simple. Dues were taken from salary checks, unless a person requested this not be done, and total dues were submitted by the school. One hundred percent NEA membership was often a school system goal. For school librarians the decision whether to join NEA or ALA presented a real quandary, for to join both was expensive. After 1924, however, there was no library department in NEA, so if one sought opportunities to lead in the school library field the desirability of ALA membership was clear. Membership also provided contacts should a librarian wish to change from school librarianship to another field in the profession.

For all these reasons, at the end of the thirties the School Libraries

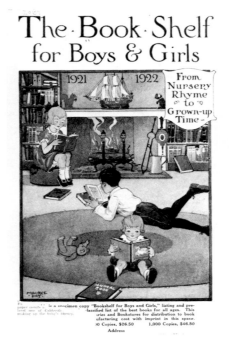

Specimen copy of Book Shelf for Boys & Girls, *1921–22, published by R. R. Bowker Company. Reprinted by permission of R. R. Bowker Company.*

Section of ALA was not only younger than the Section for Work with Children but also much weaker. It is not surprising that school library leadership was rather slow and geographically uneven in its development.

The development of leadership in the field of services for young people—teenagers—came even later. Its emergence was based on the early services for young people in three libraries: the New York Public Library, where Mabel Williams started and directed services for young people; the Cleveland Public Library, where Jean Roos headed services for youth; and the Enoch Pratt Free Library in Baltimore, where Margaret Alexander began the service in the thirties. Williams and Roos began their programs in the 1920s. Growing interest in the field encouraged Mabel Williams, and she was instrumental in organizing the ALA Young People's Reading Round Table

Book Shelf for Boys & Girls, *1922–23. Reprinted by permission of R. R. Bowker Company*

in 1930. In the thirties and forties, young people's librarians were added in a number of libraries across the country. Special courses in library schools in the area of reading for teenagers and young adults were few, however, before the 1940s.

In retrospect, the first two decades of my library life were years when children's librarians in public libraries were well recognized as a special group in the library field, when school librarians were becoming more widely involved in ALA and in demonstrating the importance of school libraries to the field of education, and when young people's service in public libraries emerged and began to spread across the country. How fortunate I was to have been there and worked with so many of these leaders.

STARTING A TREND: CHILDREN'S LIBRARIANS IN PUBLIC LIBRARIES

By 1920 public library services for children were excellent in many cities and towns across the United States, though before 1900 such services had been unusual. Many librarians had asked whether children should be admitted and allowed to borrow books. At what age? Was fourteen too young? There were few libraries where children were welcome. How was so much accomplished in such a relatively short period of time?

I believe that three remarkable women at the turn of the century were major factors in the pace of that development and in the nature and quality of children's library service in the first quarter of this century: Caroline Hewins (1846–1926), Mary Wright Plummer (1856–1916), and Lutie Eugenia Stearns (1866–1943).

In 1875 Caroline Hewins was librarian at the Young Men's Institute in Hartford, Connecticut. Her many booklists for children and talks about good children's books and the need for these to be widely available led Frederick Leypoldt, editor of *Publishers Weekly*, to ask her in 1882 to make a list of children's books. That list of more than a thousand books was quite widely distributed. It was a milestone. By 1892 the institute library, thanks to Caroline Hewins's efforts, had become the Hartford Public Library and she was the librarian. Hewins spoke at library and citizen meetings anywhere, locally or nationally. She carried on a personal campaign for good children's books in libraries and for libraries to be open to children.[1]

Mary Wright Plummer graduated in 1887, in the first class of the first library school, Melville Dewey's School of Library Economy at Columbia College in New York City. Because women were considered unacceptable on the campus of the all-male school, the school

76

moved in 1889 to Albany and became the New York State Library School. Plummer was appointed librarian of Pratt Institute in Brooklyn in 1888 and started its training school for librarians in 1890. Its library building, planned by Mary Plummer, was completed in 1896. Designed to serve the public of its Brooklyn neighborhood as well as the institute, it contained a separate children's room, an unprecedented feature.[2] Anne Carroll Moore (1871–1961), who finished her Pratt course in 1896, was the first librarian in the children's room.[3]

Plummer was an ALA vice president in 1900 when the ALA conference was held in Montreal. She had insisted that one entire session be devoted to children's work. This was the first national conference giving attention to library services for children, and before it ended, the ALA executive board was petitioned for establishment of an ALA Section for Library Work with Children. Before the end of the year, the section was established with Anne Carroll Moore as chairman and Mary Dousman (1861–1938) as secretary.[4]

Lutie E. Stearns, from Milwaukee, was teaching fourth grade there in 1886 after completing State Normal School coursework. Every Thursday night after school she, with three boys and six baskets, went by horsecar to the Milwaukee Public Library to get books for her class. Her insistence on having many library books available for teaching her classes led in 1888, on the recommendation of deputy librarian Theresa West, to Stearns's appointment as superintendent of the circulation department of the Milwaukee Public Library.[5] West (1855–1932), an important influence in American library development, served as librarian of the Milwaukee Public Library from 1892 until her marriage to Henry L. Elmendorf in 1896. They went to New York to the Buffalo Public Library in 1897, where he became librarian. Theresa West Elmendorf's library activities continued and in 1911 she became the first woman to serve as ALA president.[6]

Lutie Stearns worked for the Milwaukee Public Library from 1888 to 1897. During that time the library issued many free lists, among them *150 Good Books for Boys* and *150 Good Books for Girls*. She did a national survey of children's reading, receiving responses from 145 librarians and on which she reported both good and bad news at the 1894 ALA conference in Lake Placid. She, with Frank A. Hutchins, started the Wisconsin Free Library Commission in 1897, and she was made head of its Traveling Library Department, responsible for promoting libraries throughout the state.

In 1898 Mary Dousman (1861–1938) became a children's librarian at the Milwaukee Public Library, where she would serve as head of the children's department until 1938. She attended the Montreal ALA conference in 1900 at which the Section for Library Work with Children was organized. She was the section's first secretary, serving until 1902 along with Anne Carroll Moore, the first section chairman.[7] Moore was unable to attend the 1901 ALA conference in Waukesha, Wisconsin, and Lutie Stearns, honorary chairman, presided at the section meeting that year. Mary Dousman was elected chairman of the section for 1902–3 when the ALA conference was held at Niagara Falls.[8]

In 1906 the Wisconsin Free Library Commission established the Wisconsin Library School.[9] Other library schools were also being established at this period, and two of them specialized in the education of children's librarians. Both were originally started to train assistants for their own institutions, but almost from the beginning they attracted young women from across the country.

The Pratt Institute Library School started a second-year program for children's librarians in 1899. The example of children's services in the Pratt Institute Library children's room, as carried on by Anne Carroll Moore, was an important element in that course.[10]

At the Carnegie Library in Pittsburgh, the Training Class for Children's Librarians opened in 1900. In 1898 Edwin H. Anderson, director of the Carnegie Library, had employed Frances Jenkins Olcott (1872–1963), New York State Library School class of 1896, to organize a children's department for the main library, the branches, and the schools.[11] It could not have been many months before Frances Olcott realized that the only way to get a competent staff was to provide the training. The Carnegie Training Class for Children's Librarians, soon to be called the Training School for Children's Librarians, began with Olcott as director. She took this on in addition to her other duties.[12]

In 1903 Andrew Carnegie made a gift of five thousand dollars to the school and followed that with grants of the same amount for each of the next two years. This funding gave stability to the new school. Its roster was limited to twenty-five each year and was made up of students from across the country. When Edwin Anderson, because of health, resigned as Carnegie Library director in 1904, he

Frances Jenkins Olcott, librarian. From Public Libraries, *October 1925. Reproduced by permission.*

was replaced by Harrison Craver. In 1911 Frances Jenkins Olcott was terminated from her position at Carnegie Training School for Children's Librarians, and Sarah C. N. Bogle (1870–1932), a member of the Carnegie Library staff, became the new director. She was succeeded by Nina Brotherton, director from 1920 to 1927. From 1918 on the school prepared librarians for school and general public library as well as children's services.

It was from Pratt and Carnegie that the leaders of the twenties, thirties, and forties came. A few attended other schools but because these two gave concentrated attention to preparation for children's service, their graduates were ready and eager to make the hopes of the three remarkable women—Hewins, Plummer, and Stearns—become reality.

The 1921 ALA conference in Swampscott, Massachusetts, took place just at the end of my junior year in college. I lived only a street-car ride away from the New Ocean House, but ALA and Frederic Melcher were unknown to me. That year Alice Hazeltine (1878–

1959), head of the children's department at the St. Louis Public Library, was chairman of the Section for Library Work with Children. Frederic Melcher (1879–1963), editor of *Publishers Weekly*, had an idea. He had long been interested in children's books. He talked with the children's librarians' section about a possible medal to encourage children's book authors, and he proposed such an award to the ALA Executive Board, adding that if accepted he would have an appropriate medal designed and struck off each year to present to the winner. The proposal was enthusiastically accepted and the section was given responsibility for making the selection of the winning book each year. After I became a children's librarian and learned of the events at Swampscott, how I wished I had attended that 1921 meeting of the ALA!

Clara Whitehill Hunt (1871–1958), superintendent of the children's department at the Brooklyn Public Library from 1903 to 1940, was chairman of the Section for Library Work with Children for the ALA conference in Detroit in 1922. This was the year that Melcher's idea became a reality. The Newbery Medal had been sculpted, the medal for the first winner had been struck off, and it was given to Clara Hunt for presentation to the first winner, Hendrik Van Loon, for his *Story of Mankind* (Boni & Liveright, 1921). In 1900, Clara Hunt had attended the meeting of the ALA in Montreal. She was chairman of the section for both the 1904 St. Louis and 1905 Portland conferences.[13] She had begun her library career in Brooklyn in 1903, and she retired about 1940.

At the end of my second year at library school in 1924, I applied for the position of head of the children's department at the Omaha Public Library. The librarian there, Edith Tobitt (1868–1939), wrote to set up an interview and said she and the president of the library board "were both amused at what you say in your letter regarding the distance. I want to call to your mind that Omaha is in the center of the United States, also that the people here mostly come from your own locality. I hope that if you come to the middle west to accept a library position that you will not find it strange."[14] So, no question, I was a provincial New Englander. I thoroughly enjoyed the people in Omaha and knew before I had been there long how lucky I was to be working with Edith Tobitt, an excellent public librarian in any decade.

After three years there I went to the State Teachers College in St. Cloud, Minnesota, to be the first children's librarian in a teachers college in that state. No children's or school librarian could have had a more productive experience as a basis for helping teachers to know children's books and letting them see how essential good library service is to good teaching.

The next year, in 1928, I went to Evanston, Illinois, to be librarian at Haven School, a combined elementary and junior high school. I was fortunate in being able to work with a gifted principal. The opportunities to experiment with what I had learned at the teachers college were many, and my eight years at Haven were perpetually stimulating.

In 1936 I went to ALA to work in the school and children's library division, and from that date on I came to know and work with large numbers of librarians in the children's and school library field. But, of course, by then I was an ALA member and had attended three ALA conferences—in 1924, 1926, and 1927—so I had already seen and heard some of the outstanding librarians of the twenties. Some I came to know well, others I knew but slightly. I can give only a glimpse of each.

Anne Carroll Moore, Pratt class of 1896, was first superintendent of work with children at the New York Public Library. From her initial appointment in 1906 until her retirement in 1941 she was an energetic and individualistic leader. Moore's involvement in reviewing books for children, in a personal and distinctive way, made her known throughout the country. First there was her monthly column on children's books in the *Bookman* (1918–24). Then her reviews appeared on the weekly "Three Owls" page in the New York *Herald Tribune*'s "Books" (1924–30). Many of these reviews were collected in her Three Owls books. From 1936 through 1960 the *Horn Book* carried her reviews.[15]

OUTSTANDING
CHILDREN'S
LIBRARIANS
OF THE 1920S

New York City was then as now the center of children's book publishing, and thus Anne Carroll Moore was often consulted by children's book editors and publishers. Her reactions were appreciated and often acted upon. At times she could be caustic in reviews and in comments, but she was never colorless. Stories about her are legion but I do have one to add.

In the thirties Priscilla Edie (later, Morton) (b. 1899) was children's librarian at the 135th Street Branch. (Augusta Baker, then in her

Anne Carroll Moore in the Children's Room of the New York Public Library. From Frances Clarke Sayers, Anne Carroll Moore, *copyright ©
1972 Frances Clarke Sayers. Reproduced by permission of
Atheneum Publishers, Inc.*

twenties, began her New York Public Library experience as Edie's
assistant children's librarian.) One day after Moore and Ruth Hill
(later, Viguers) (1903–1971) had come to the branch to solve some
problem, they and Priscilla Edie took a taxi to return downtown.
Anne Carroll Moore suddenly remembered that one of Wagner's op-
eras was being done at the Met that day. They turned on the radio
and then rode for hours through Central Park until the broadcast of
the opera was over. The taxi driver thought they were crazy. Later
Priscilla Edie confessed that she did not remember the particular
Wagner or the singers, but she said she would never forget the impression it made as they rode through the trees and past the lakes
listening to that glorious music.[16]

Alice Jordan (1870–1960) was appointed a children's librarian in
the central children's room at the Boston Public Library in 1902. She

was made head of the children's department in 1917 and served until her retirement in 1941. She was chairman of the Section for Library Work with Children in 1907 for the ALA conference in Asheville, North Carolina, and again for the Louisville conference in 1917.

In 1906 Alice Jordan invited thirteen librarians from greater Boston to meet at the library to talk about books and library services for children. The meeting had been planned because library assistants wished to have the opportunity to exchange ideas and to talk freely about their problems and procedures. This was not possible at general library meetings. The quarterly meetings were chaired until 1914 by Jordan, and librarians came from further and further afield to attend. Then the group decided to organize and elect a chairman, and it became the New England Round Table of Children's Librarians.[17] Talk about books was always a major part of the meetings. From at least 1916 on members were continuously evaluating books and editions for a list of classics. Resulting lists were mimeographed and made available periodically, but their distribution was limited. In February 1947, however, the *Horn Book* published Jordan's excellent "Children's Classics," reprinting the essay in pamphlet format and appending a list of the classics in recommended editions.

As parent-teacher organizations were established in a growing number of communities across the country, children's librarians helped their members become acquainted with children's books. At the national level Alice Jordan was probably the first to cooperate with the National Congress of Parents and Teachers (NCPT). She served as chairman of the NCPT's Children's Book Committee from 1914 through 1922.

Jordan was also an important resource for Bertha Mahony (1882–1969) as she prepared to establish The Bookshop for Boys and Girls in Boston in 1916. She guided Bertha Mahony in learning to know children's books with a series of Saturday assignments and discussions and list makings. Mahony used lists by Caroline Hewins and Clara Hunt as well as advice from Frederic Melcher, then in the bookstore business himself, too. Jordan was again helpful to Bertha Mahony when she and Elinor Whitney started *Horn Book Magazine* from the Bookshop in 1924. It was the first periodical devoted entirely to children's books and it is now celebrating its sixtieth anniversary.

The Boston Public Library's Alice M. Jordan Collection is a valuable resource for historical research on nineteenth- and twentieth-century literature for children, on library service to children, and on Jordan's long and significant career. It is good news that this most important collection now has a curator, Mary Beth Dunhouse.

Gertrude Andrus (1880–1970), Carnegie 1904, went to the Seattle Public Library in 1908 as the first trained librarian to head its children's department, which opened in 1891. In 1916 Andrus chaired the ALA Section for Library Work with Children when the conference was in Asbury Park, New Jersey. Three years later, she took a year's leave to start a children's book department for Frederick and Nelson, the large Seattle department store owned by Marshall Field. Rather than returning to the library when the year was out, Andrus stayed to run the book department until 1940! I wonder if she was, perhaps, the first children's librarian to manage a bookstore. She did return to the Seattle Public Library after leaving Frederick and Nelson and headed the children's department there until 1946.[18]

Elva S. Smith (1871–1965), Carnegie 1902, taught in the school. In 1925 she became head of the Carnegie Library Children's Department. In 1923 Elva Smith was chairman of the Section for Library Work with Children at the ALA conference in Hot Springs, Arkansas, and presented the second Newbery Medal to Hugh Lofting for *The Voyages of Doctor Dolittle* (Frederick A. Stokes, 1922).

In 1909 a young woman from Washington State arrived in Pittsburgh and presented herself at the Training School ready to take the course. She was Jasmine Britton (1886–1979). She had no place to stay. The letter she had sent had not arrived. Could she stay? The faculty took her in and that first night, according to the story, she slept crosswise on Elva Smith's bed, as presumably Smith did, too.[19] Britton completed her work in 1910 and she went to California to organize children's work at the Los Angeles Public Library in 1916. The Los Angeles City Schools appointed her head of their Library and Textbook Section and supervisor of school libraries and she was an outstanding school library leader there from 1920 until her retirement in 1950.

Effie L. Power (1873–1969) entered the field of library service to children in 1895, only three years after she graduated from high school. William Howard Brett (1884–1918), librarian of the Cleveland Public Library from 1884 to 1918, employed her as an apprentice for three months without pay to see if she would work out. She

Children's Books for General Reading

Selected by

EFFIE L. POWER

for the

Children's Librarians Section
of the A. L. A.

Second edition

CHICAGO
AMERICAN LIBRARY ASSOCIATION
1929

Children's Books for General Reading, *selected by Effie L. Power*
(Chicago: American Library Association, 1929).

was Cleveland Public Library's first children's librarian, working from an alcove in the central library with the books on closed shelves, available to children only over the counter. By 1898 there was a children's room in the central library. Effie Power attended the 1900 ALA conference in Montreal at which the Section for Library Work with Children was established.[20]

In 1903 she went to Carnegie and, following her course, became an instructor in library use at the Cleveland City Normal School. After leaving the Normal School position in 1909 she was in the children's department and teaching in the library school at Pittsburgh's Carnegie Library and then at the St. Louis Public Library.[21] In 1913 Power served as chairman of the children's librarians section for the ALA Kaaterskill, New York, conference.

In 1904 Caroline Burnite (Walker) (1875–1936), Pratt Library School 1904, became the head of the children's department at the Cleveland Public Library where she was outstanding in developing citywide services to children. In 1920 Power returned to Cleveland Public, this time to head the children's department. At the 1930 ALA conference in Los Angeles Power was again chairman of the section. The Newbery Medal winner for that year was Rachel Field for *Hitty, Her First Hundred Years* (A Louise Seaman Book, Macmillan, 1929). Rosemary Livsey (b. 1898), who was then head of the Los Angeles Public Library central children's room and a hostess for the conference, remembers that Hitty came out to the conference from New York by plane. Rosemary Livsey and a small party went by plane to meet Hitty in midair. "Rachel Field, on the westbound plane sent her greetings over the air to our plane," reported Livsey.[22] In the May 1950 issue of *Top of the News* which recognized the fiftieth anniversary of the ALA section, Effie Power recalled Hitty's dramatic arrival to receive her medal.[23]

I first met Effie Power when I went to Cleveland in the spring of 1923 for the New York State Library School's required month of practice work. She had organized my schedule so that it included opportunities to work a little in every activity area. The library was still located on several floors of a building on Euclid Avenue near the Public Square. Before I left, Linda Eastman (d. 1963), the librarian, took time to show me and a colleague the plans for the building to be constructed on Superior Street.

I have treasured memories of that privilege and of the many other librarians I met that month, especially Annie Spencer Cutter (1877–1957), who headed the school department, and Elizabeth Briggs (1888–1953), head of the central children's room, who would succeed Power in 1937. That month was a determining point in my library career. It showed me ideal library service for children. It showed me what it was like to be part of a professional and cooperative staff where each person at every level was involved in working to achieve the very best possible service for the library's community.

The next year I had special reason to be grateful to Effie Power. When I applied for the position of head of the children's department in Omaha, I had no library experience and a reference was considered essential. In desperation, I suggested the Cleveland librarian might say something about me to my potential employer. She did— that I would be a good gamble. Anyway, I got the job.

Mary Wilkinson (b. 1897) began her training at Carnegie in the fall of 1910. Frances Jenkins Olcott, the director, considered interrupting the course to take a position to be desirable because of the experience gained. So in February 1911 Wilkinson was, as she said, "booted out" to fill a position in Superior, Wisconsin.[24] That led to a position in St. Louis for four years and it was 1917 before she returned to Pittsburgh to complete her course, spending half time in classes and half time as librarian of Schenley High School.

In a recent letter Mary Wilkinson, who is now in her nineties, recalled her Newbery Medal experience in 1925. She was children's librarian at the Hackley Public Library in Muskegon, Michigan, when she served as chairman of the ALA Section for Library Work with Children. The ALA conference was held in Seattle that year. She was to present the fourth medal to Charles Finger for *Tales from Silver Lands* (Doubleday, 1924). The university room in which this presentation was assigned to occur was much too small for the crowd. Sarah C. N. Bogle (1870–1932), by then ALA assistant executive secretary and a commanding figure of ample proportions, could scarcely squeeze through the door. Charles Finger could not reach the platform. What to do? Fortunately, outside there was a sort of shallow bowl on the campus lawn. Mary Wilkinson announced that the meeting would reconvene outdoors. Sarah Bogle let out her breath. Charles Finger was escorted outside. People seated themselves on the grass. The award was presented and accepted. Then came lunch, an outdoor buffet. Several people, however, wanted to talk to the author and this took a little time. When Wilkinson, Finger, and the other special guests reached the tables not a crumb was left! Nonplussed, Wilkinson decided to take her several guests downtown for lunch. But how to get there? A lady standing nearby offered her car and that of a friend. Off the party went. The driver was not a librarian but was interested in children and reading and insisted that all of Wilkinson's guests be her guests at an elegant luncheon. Afterward Charles Finger took Mary Wilkinson for a boat ride on Puget Sound and as they went round and round the sound, he regaled her with stories of his adventurous life. On the whole, she said, it was the most *interesting* ALA she ever attended.[25]

In 1926 Joseph L. Wheeler (1884–1970) was appointed librarian of Baltimore's Enoch Pratt Free Library and charged with bringing it into the twentieth century. To help in this monumental task, he appointed Mary Wilkinson to direct work with children and she arrived in January 1927. Before the end of that year a bond issue for a new building had been passed and many steps toward developing modern library service were being taken.

Describing what was done first in the children's department, Wilkinson says, "Two pressing needs had to be met: First, more and better books, and, second, a staff, informed and enthusiastic about books. We began with weekly meetings of one assistant from each branch and one from the children's room. Here we talked about individual books, ways of presenting them, about authors, about differences in children—at times with lively discussions. . . . We were fortunate in our visitors. May Massee from Doubleday, Virginia Kirkus then of Harper, and Louise Seaman from Macmillan excited the group with their adventures in publishing children's books. Alice Jordan from Boston Public Library, Ethel Bubb from Washington, and Anne Carroll Moore from New York encouraged and thrilled them with talks of their work with children."[26]

When I first visited the Enoch Pratt Free Library in the late thirties or early forties it was hard to believe the children's department had ever been other than outstanding. Mary Wilkinson, with firm and imaginative leadership and a quiet sense of humor, had accomplished wonders. With Joseph Wheeler's support, she had assembled a splendid staff and a well-chosen book collection. Her program was tailored to meet the needs of Baltimore children.

Lillian H. Smith (1887–1983) and Mary Wilkinson began their Carnegie Training School courses together in the fall of 1910 and were roommates there. Lillian Smith completed her course in 1911, was recommended to Anne Carroll Moore, and began her career at the New York Public Library (NYPL) children's department that fall. The next spring George Locke, chief librarian for Toronto Public Library, inquired about the Canadian on the NYPL staff and approached Smith about organizing a children's department for that library. She accepted and began her work in Toronto in September 1912, becoming "the first trained children's librarian in the British Empire."[27]

I first met Lillian Smith in the summer of 1925 following my first year in Omaha. I stopped over in Toronto on my way home to Massachusetts. The Victorian Boys and Girls House next door to the Library was unusual, certainly, but attractive and inviting. I asked for Smith and was taken upstairs to her small, unpretentious office, transformed from a bedroom. She had tea brought in. I am not sure which of us was more shy. I sensed intense reserve and at the same time warm friendliness and quiet humor.

Later, as I came to know more of her leadership and of her training via weekly staff meetings, I was impressed with the way she helped the staff develop a rich knowledge of literature and of the sources and versions of tales, legends, and myths which become the resources for library storytelling. When I was leaving Omaha in 1927, I approached Lillian Smith about coming to Toronto to work so that I might benefit from that staff training. That would not be possible, she said, for salaries there were very low and only young women living at home with their families could afford to work at Boys and Girls House.

She had a talent for inspiring those who worked with her not only in the library but in contacts throughout the provinces and in professional associations. I marveled at the time and generosity of her responses to the hundreds of letters asking for help. They came from all over Canada. Before there was a Canadian Library Association (which she helped organize in 1953) she was a one woman national library adviser on children's books. Letters, often from some small place of which she had never heard, brought requests for lists of books to buy or questions about what books to buy for fifty or one hundred dollars. Sometimes the money was enclosed! She re-

89

sponded with individually tailored lists, advised on how to buy and where to get books, and on some occasions bought the books herself for her correspondents. Many children in small towns and villages across Canada thus had the chance to read good books that without her advice and assistance might not have come their way.

All this was done in addition to Smith's demanding children's department responsibilities and her activities in professional organizations. She founded the Canadian Association of Children's Librarians in 1937. She was chairman of the ALA Section for Library Work with Children for the 1924 conference in Saratoga Springs at which Mrs. Charles B. Hawes accepted her late husband's Newbery Medal for *The Dark Frigate* (Little, Brown, 1923). She chaired the Children's Library Association (the section's new name after an ALA reorganization) in 1942–43 when there was no ALA conference because of the war. The children's librarians in the New York area rallied, however, and there was a dinner for some 275 people at the Roosevelt Hotel in New York on June 14, 1943. Lillian Smith was there to present the Newbery Medal to Elizabeth Vining for *Adam of the Road* (Viking, 1942) and the Caldecott Medal to Virginia Lee Burton for her illustrations in *The Little House* (Houghton, Mifflin, 1942).

Julia Carter (1884–1980), Pratt 1906, was New York Public Library children's librarian from 1907 to 1924. Afterward, she was supervisor of work with children at the Cincinnati Public Library from 1927 until well into the 1950s. She became a children's library leader not only in the city but in Ohio and the region, and she was much involved in ALA activities. Several from her well-trained staff went on to provide leadership in other children's departments. Among them, Marion Young (1908–1985) headed the department in Detroit and Mary Peters (b. 1911) went to Cleveland Public. Carter was chairman of the section at the 1938 conference in Kansas City when Kate Seredy received the Newbery Medal for *White Stag* (Viking, 1937) and Dorothy Lathrop received the first Caldecott Medal for *Animals of the Bible*, edited by Helen Dean Fish for Frederick A. Stokes.

Della McGregor (1889–1978) went to library school at the University of Wisconsin in 1911. She became a children's librarian in the St. Paul Public Library and, after a course at the Carnegie Library School in Pittsburgh, became chief of the children's department in St. Paul from 1916 to her retirement in 1961. For many of those years she also taught at the University of Minnesota Library School. By 1939 she had planned and opened the Memorial Skinner Room for Young People. There were only a few special rooms for young people in public libraries at this time (Cleveland Public had its Robert Louis Stevenson Room from the opening of the new building in 1925) but it was a feature which would become more common in later decades.

In 1931–32 Della McGregor served as chairman of the Newbery Medal Committee and the book selected for the medal was *Waterless Mountain* (Longmans, 1931) by Laura Armer. The ALA conference was in New Orleans that year and it was the chairman's idea that the award should be presented at a Newbery Medal dinner. The following year in Chicago when she was chairman of the ALA section she named it the Newbery Medal Banquet, and so it was called through the years.

The Newbery Dinner held at the Hotel Pierre in New York City, 1937.

May Massee (1883–1966) completed the Wisconsin Free Library Commission summer course in 1903. (After the Wisconsin Library School's establishment in 1906, those who had taken the earlier eight-week summer course were considered "trained" by the commission.) In 1905 she went to the Buffalo Public Library, where she soon became head of the children's department. She remained there through 1909.[28] As chairman of the ALA Section for Library Work with Children in 1909–10 she presided at the ALA Mackinac Island conference. She went to the American Library Association headquarters to edit the *Booklist* in 1913. She left the library field for publishing in 1922, becoming Doubleday, Doran's second children's book editor.[29] The first editor was Louise Seaman (later Bechtel) (1894–1985) who began her list at Macmillan in 1919. May Massee was not the only librarian to become an editor. Marian Fiery went from New York Public Library to E. P. Dutton in 1925 and Bertha Gunterman, also a librarian, went to edit children's books at Longmans, Green. Other early editors were Helen Dean Fish at Frederick A. Stokes, Virginia Kirkus at Harper, and Lucile Gulliver at Little, Brown.

Louise P. Latimer (1879–1962), Carnegie class of 1911, went directly to the District of Columbia Public Library in Washington, first heading the children's department's work with schools. In 1919 she was made head of the department, and she continued her work there until late in the 1940s. Latimer was chairman of the ALA section at the 1927 conference in Toronto. At that meeting, however, it is Anne Carroll Moore rather than Louise Latimer whom I remember. Someone spoke up from the back of the room. It was a compelling voice, firm, speaking very deliberately, and with quiet authority. The chairman called her by name, Miss Moore. So this was the famous Anne Carroll Moore, I thought. I turned to see her. She had on a dull red dress and was not at her best. I decided she looked like a witch. It was some years before I met her, and, although not a witch, she certainly had a magic about her. Later on, I met with her a number of times, but even now it is her voice that I remember most vividly.

Early in her career Louise Latimer became interested in illustrated children's books and began the District of Columbia library's outstanding collection. In 1929 Faxon published her *Illustrators: A Finding List.* The collection kept growing and became a major re-

Anne Carroll Moore (left) and Lillian H. Smith celebrating the publication of The Art of Beatrix Potter *(London and New York: F. Warne, [1955]) during a visit to the Osborne Collection, Toronto Public Library, 1955. Courtesy of the Osborne Collection, Toronto. The book contains an appreciation written by Anne Carroll Moore.*

source for the preparation of the *Illustrators of Children's Books* (Horn Book, 1947) by Bertha Mahony, Louise Latimer, and Beulah Folmsbee, a beautiful and tremendously useful first book of its kind.

Elizabeth Nesbitt (1897–1977) was in the Pittsburgh Carnegie Library children's department from 1922 and served as supervisor of storytelling there until 1926. From 1929 throughout the 1930s and beyond she taught in Carnegie Library School. She was a master storyteller and her talks on storytelling at library meetings were memorable.

Named in her honor is the Elizabeth Nesbitt Room at the University of Pittsburgh School of Library and Information Science, which houses the extensive historical collection of children's books begun in the days of Frances Jenkins Olcott and Elva S. Smith. Today in the Nesbitt Room is the beginning of an archive of the history and development of children's library service in this country. A national center for the history of children's libraries and children's librarianship is most appropriate in the school which grew out of the Carnegie Library Training Class for Children's Librarians of 1900.

Charlemae Rollins (1897–1979) became children's librarian at the Hall Branch of Chicago Public Library in 1932 after she returned from her training at Columbia University School of Library Service. She was already critical of children's books in which black children were portrayed as servants or as inferiors, books often written in false dialect which seemed to be intended to be humorous. At meetings of teachers and of librarians she made clear the effects of these thoughtless books on black children. She pleaded with publishers, authors, and illustrators to make good books with respect for black children, honest, contemporary books about these youngsters. She outlined guidelines for such books and made lists of acceptable books with black characters. Gradually librarians, teachers, and publishers began to recognize and weed out poor books which would not meet Charlemae Rollins's standards. New books appeared by black authors and others with genuine characters with which black children could happily identify. Rollins's pamphlet *We Build Together: A Reader's Guide to Negro Life and Literature for Elementary and High School Use* (National Council of Teachers of English, 1941) brought awareness to many people throughout the country of a long-standing insensitivity among adults who created books or used them with children.

Jessie Gay Van Cleve (1880–1944), Carnegie 1913, was from Michigan and extolled its charms all her life. In 1922 she came to ALA headquarters to join the *Booklist* staff, selecting and annotating the children's books to be recommended. Also coming to ALA at that time were Carl Milam (1884–1963), who served as executive secretary, and Sara C. N. Bogle, assistant executive secretary. Jessie Van Cleve continued there from 1922 until her retirement in 1937. After coming to ALA Van Cleve became well known in the Chicago area, and by 1932 she, Agatha Shea (1893–1955), and Adah Whitcomb of the Chicago Public Library organized the Chicago Children's Reading Round Table with Van Cleve as its first president. The Round Table has continued, now as in the beginning, to include librarians, teachers, authors, booksellers, reviewers, and publishers.

I expect I became acquainted with Jessie Van Cleve about the time the Round Table was begun. Like everyone else, I enjoyed her humor, her tale-telling, and her enthusiasm for children's books.

In 1936 she and I became the staff of the long-sought ALA office to represent the interests of librarians working with children in public and school libraries. Jessie Van Cleve was chief of this new ALA School and Children's Library Division and also its children's library specialist. I was the rest of the professional staff, designated school library specialist. We worked half time in the division and half time doing the children's books for the *Booklist*. That was not all. We went together to Cleveland Public Library to meet with the children's and school librarians and to Detroit to meet with Board of Education school librarians and Public Library children's librarians. We had an extended Louisiana trip led by state school Library Commission personnel. Our last trip before her illness was in the spring of 1937 to a number of New York libraries, public and school, with Anna Kennedy (1891–1984), state school library supervisor. It was a professionally exhilarating two years and to become well acquainted with Jessie Van Cleve was a personal joy. When she left, I was alone. I was relieved of *Booklist* responsibilities and for some years was the division staff, children's and school library specialist.

A word or two about book selection aids for libraries. In 1904 the *Booklist*, a monthly book reviewing journal for libraries, was established at ALA. For many years larger libraries (in which books were seen before or soon after publication) cooperated by indicating on frequent lists sent out from the *Booklist* those books which they deemed desirable or undesirable for library purchase. The compilation of these "votes" was advisory to the *Booklist* staff, who determined which books would be recommended in the publication.

BOOK
SELECTION
AND
SELECTION
AIDS

Other aids in library selection were periodic lists from state library agencies such as those from the Wisconsin Free Library Commission and large library lists such as the Cleveland Public Library's *Open Shelf*, available on subscription.

Another list, especially for smaller libraries, came periodically from the H. R. Huntting Company in Springfield, Massachusetts. The need to rebind children's books was a problem for libraries.

95

Some books would circulate only eight or ten times before rebinding was required, and then it would be months before they were returned and back in use. So prebinding, a service which Huntting introduced before 1920, was most welcome. Well selected and annotated lists of children's books, developed by a group of children's librarians, were widely circulated and books included could all be purchased prebound. Near the end of the 1920s the New Method Book Bindery in Jacksonville, Illinois, also began providing prebound children's books.

The *ALA Catalog*, first published in 1904, and the *Children's Catalog* of the H. W. Wilson Company, which began in 1909, came out in updated editions at intervals of several years. Both were ideal for checking children's book collections, for selecting editions, and for locating books on specific subjects.

In the 1920s and 1930s publishers had "backlists." A book published five years earlier would be maintained in stock and would continue to be available. Standard classics could be selected or replaced in several editions with different illustrators and formats. New editions of favorite books were being printed. In the twenties at Macmillan Louise Seaman began her Children's Classics editions, thirty or forty of them, matching outstanding authors with a variety of fine illustrators. The books were well designed and well bound, and they had attractively designed covers; they sold for $1.75 each. Bechtel also published a series of twenty-five or thirty hard bound Little Library books priced at $1.00 each. These were a pleasure for middle graders to hold and read, and what an array of titles and illustrators they included! Children's library shelves were becoming more interesting and inviting.

No one was yet doing books for beginning readers. Bertha Mahony, in her comprehensive and helpful *Realms of Gold* (Doubleday, Doran, 1929), had to include textbook primers and readers as did librarians throughout the 1930s in order to have anything at all for children just beginning to read. How different that is today!

MORE CHILDREN'S LIBRARY LEADERS

Carrie Scott (1874–1943), New York State Library School 1906, Carnegie 1907, was supervisor of children's work for the Indianapolis Public Library from 1917 until her death. I visited there in 1925 and was taken to meet the librarian, Charles Rush. By way of conversation he asked about the Omaha Public Library where I was then employed. What was its budget? I had no idea. My response brought a reprimand. I *should* know the budget! Charles Rush's question prompted my early realization that children's librarians cannot operate in their own separate worlds but must see themselves as participating members of the library staff and must make certain that the staff and board perceive them as such.

Carrie Scott chaired the Section for Library Work with Children at the 1929 ALA conference held in Washington, D.C., when the Newbery Medal was given to Eric Kelly for *The Trumpeter of Krakow* (Macmillan, 1928). Scott was short and a bit on the round side, rather a dumpling of a person. She and Edna Johnson of the University of Indiana faculty compiled the *Anthology of Children's Literature* (Houghton Mifflin, 1935). It was one of the early anthologies of children's literature, to be followed by many others, which were widely used in children's literature classes.

Nina Brotherton (1884–1949), Western Reserve 1907, worked at the Cleveland Public Library as a children's librarian until 1912. A course she took that year with the famous Norwegian storyteller Gudrun Thorne-Thomsen led to her appointment as director of storytelling, a position she held until 1917. From Cleveland she went to Pittsburgh in 1920 to be principal of the Carnegie Library School. In 1926 at the ALA fiftieth anniversary conference in Atlantic City, Brotherton was chairman of the section. The Newbery Medal that year went to Arthur Chrisman for *Shen of the Sea* (E. P. Dutton, 1925).

In 1927 Nina Brotherton went to Boston to join the faculty at Simmons College School of Library Science, and she remained there until her death in 1949. Her interest throughout her teaching career was in children's library service and in storytelling. Although I saw her at ALA conferences, I was seldom able to go to New England meetings and therefore did not come to know her personally.

Elizabeth Knapp (1894–1931) began her library career in the children's department of the Detroit Public Library in 1914. At the ALA Colorado Springs Conference in 1920 she was chairman of the Section for Library Work with Children. In 1925 she was made Detroit's first head of children's services, where she served until her sudden death in 1931. She organized that library's excellent services to children and was highly regarded. The Elizabeth Knapp Branch Library, which opened in 1950, was named in her honor. Also as a memorial to her, a talented Detroit sculptor in the Federal Art Project made a delightful sculpture of two children curled up listening to "Little Thumb," which was placed in the central library children's room.

Vera Prout (d. 1960), Carnegie 1914, was a Detroit Public Library children's librarian who served as storytelling specialist for several years. In 1924 she was appointed to head the children's department at the Kansas City Public Library (Missouri) where she worked until 1955. In the early years in Kansas City she taught a training class for children's librarians. A student in the training class was Jean Merrill who became an assistant in the main children's room through the 1930s and after further training returned to succeed Vera Prout as head of the department. Peggy Sullivan began her career as a children's librarian in 1952 in Vera Prout's department before moving on to the Enoch Pratt Free Library in Baltimore.

Harriet Leaf (b. 1892), Carnegie 1915, was an instructor at the school and worked in the Carnegie Library in various posts from 1915 to 1925. She was at the Cleveland Public Library from 1926 to 1928. She was then named director, later coordinator, of the Akron Public Library children's department, a position which she held until the late 1950s. She was active as a leader in the Ohio libraries and in ALA. At the ALA Buffalo conference in 1946 she presented the Newbery Medal to Robert Lawson for *Rabbit Hill* (Viking, 1948) and the Caldecott Medal to Maud and Miska Petersham for *The Rooster Crows* (Macmillan, 1948).

Helen Martin (1889–1943), Carnegie 1911–16, worked during her course in the Carnegie Library children's department. She then went to the East Cleveland Public Library as children's librarian. She studied at Western Reserve University Library School and was on the faculty there for a number of years. The *ALA Bulletin* for April 1931 carried her article "Good Reading for Children: A Retrospect of ALA Accomplishments and a Prospect of Work to Be Done." It was an excellent summary of early twentieth-century children's service. Martin went on to study at the Graduate Library School at the University of Chicago, receiving her Ph.D. in 1934. Her dissertation on "Internationalism in Children's Books," was, I believe, the first doctoral study in the field.

Gladys English (1886–1956), Western Reserve 1917, held numerous posts in California. She first headed the school department at Fresno County Library (1918–21), then became assistant at the Berkeley Public Library (1921–22), was on the staff of Mills College

(1922–23), became librarian of Tuolumne County Library (1923–24), and served as librarian at Piedmont High School (1924–26, 1927–30) with a year out (1926–27) to serve as ALA headquarters librarian in Chicago. In 1930 she went to the Los Angeles Public Library to be department librarian for work with children and she continued in that position until 1950.

The year Gladys English was chairman of the ALA Section for Library Work with Children and the conference took place in San Francisco, she presented the Newbery Medal to Elizabeth Enright for *Thimble Summer* (Holt, Rinehart, and Winston, 1938) and the Caldecott Medal to Thomas Handforth for *Mei Li* (Doubleday, 1938). Two years before, in 1937, she had begun editing a quarterly *Newsletter* for the section. When the section was combined with the School Libraries Section and the Young People's Reading Round Table to become the ALA Division of Libraries for Children and Young People, the *Newsletter* was offered to the new division and accepted. Its name was changed to *Top of the News* and Gladys English was its first editor, serving from October 1942 until June 1944.

Harriet Long (b. 1897) attended the training class for children's librarians in the 1920s that was given by Ethel C. Wright, head of the children's department (who had been in the 1909 Carnegie Training School class) at the Toledo Public Library. Long went to the Albany Public Library in 1924 to head its children's department. That year Albany opened its first central building, the Harmanus Bleeker Library. Leaving New York, Long worked in the Cleveland Public Library's Lewis Carroll Room from 1926 to 1930 and at the same time studied at Western Reserve University Library School. After receiving her degree in 1939, she joined Western Reserve's library school faculty, where she taught in the area of children's librarianship for the next fifteen years.

Harriet Long chaired the Section for Library Work with Children in 1943–44, when there was no ALA conference because of the war. Children's librarians who could get there attended a luncheon in Cleveland at which she presented the Newbery Medal to Esther Forbes for *Johnny Tremain* (Houghton, Mifflin, 1943) and the Caldecott Medal to Louis Slobodkin for his illustrations for *Many Moons* (Harcourt, Brace, 1943), written by James Thurber. Harriet Long wrote *Rich the Treasure: Public Library Service to Children*, which was published by ALA in 1953.

My second position after Omaha Public Library was the State Teachers College in St. Cloud, Minnesota, in 1927–28. Harriet Wood (1871–1937), state supervisor of school libraries in the Minnesota Department of Public Instruction, wanted teachers colleges to include a children's librarian on their practice school or college library staffs. She persuaded St. Cloud to add such a position, suggesting me for it. I was the first children's librarian in a Minnesota teachers college, although I had never taken any courses in education or considered teaching as a career.

That year really taught me something about the relationship of school libraries to teaching. The practice school teachers were masters of their craft. They welcomed what children's books and a children's library could do to enrich teaching and saw to it that their practice teachers used the library, sought my help, and also brought boys and girls to the library to work with them there. The subject teachers in the colleges, especially the geography teacher and the rural education teacher, periodically asked for an introduction to children's books on the subjects they had been covering. It was a rewarding experience for me and a tremendous help in understanding teacher needs when I became an elementary school librarian in 1928.

My St. Cloud year demonstrated to me how important practice school libraries and librarians could be in teacher training institutions. When I went to work at ALA in 1936 the influence of practice schools on school library progress was still on my mind.

In 1939–40 Gretchen Westervelt (b. 1889), elementary school librarian at the Potsdam State Teachers College in New York, was ALA School Libraries Section Chairman. She planned a preconference for the 1940 ALA Cincinnati conference on practice or demonstration school libraries. Participants would share experiences and consider their relationship to progress in school library development and their responsibilities for it. Many of the practice school librarians whom I knew to have been outstanding during the years 1936–40 were at the preconference: Anne Thaxter Eaton (1881–1971), Lincoln School, Teachers College, Columbia University, 1917–42; Irene Hayner (b. 1896), University High School, University of Michigan, 1927–45; Frieda Heller (b. 1897), Demonstration School, Ohio State University, 1932 into the 1950s or 1960s; Ruth Ersted (b. 1904), University High School, University of Minnesota, 1933–36; Thelma Eaton, Milne High School, New York State Teachers College, Albany, 1933–42; Miriam Snow Mathes (b. 1905), Campus School, West Washington State Teachers College, Bellingham, 1934 into the late 1940s or early 1950s; Jessie Boyd (1899–1978), University High School, University of California, Oakland, 1936–47; Frances Henne (b. 1906), University High School, University of Chicago, 1939–42; and Sarita Davis (1905–1969), Elementary School, University of Michigan, 1939–49.

Nora Beust, who received a certificate from the Wisconsin Library School in 1913, joined the Cleveland Public Library's Training Class the next year. After two years on the staff of the Wisconsin State Teachers College Library in La Crosse, she became children's librarian at the La Crosse Public Library. In 1927 she began work as librarian at the School of Education at the University of North Carolina. Following receipt of her M.A. in 1929 she became a member of the university's Library School faculty and taught there until 1937. Her major interest and attention was in the area of training children's librarians. In 1930 and again in 1936 she compiled the *Graded List of Books for Children* published by ALA. This list had been developed by an ALA committee chaired by Annie Spencer Cutter (Cleveland Public Library). Committee members included Nina C. Brotherton (Carnegie Library School), Jasmine Britton (Los Angeles City Schools), Anne Thaxter Eaton (Lincoln School, Columbia University), and John Adams Lowe (Brooklyn Public Library).

My first experience with Nora Beust was decisive for her and for me. Sometime in 1935 the U.S. Office of Education announced a civil service examination for a new staff position, specialist in school and children's libraries. Both Nora Beust and I took the exam. She got the job. Before the announcement of the results, I was appointed to the staff of ALA's new School and Children's Library Division. Becoming school library specialist at ALA in 1936 was an exciting opportunity and for that job I could continue living in Evanston.

In 1924 I went to Haven School, a junior high and elementary school in Evanston, Illinois, as librarian. Ida Faye Wright (1880–1974) was librarian of the Evanston Public Library, and in 1922 she brought Edith Moon (1877–1950), Carnegie Training School 1912–13, to Evanston to organize school library service in the elementary schools. (The high school in Evanston is a separate school district.)

It was to be a cooperative program supported jointly by the public library and the public schools. By 1928 this plan was well established. The two schools for seventh and eighth grades had full-time librarians who worked school hours. All the lower schools had library rooms and trained librarians, some part-time in the early years. Funds for books and salaries of librarians were shared. Books were purchased through the public library and cataloged by a special cataloger for the school libraries. Haven School's library served as a public library branch two afternoons and evenings each week, and for this there was a special staff. But this was the only one of the school libraries also used as a branch. The school librarians worked under the supervision of Gertrude Morse (1891–1958), the head of children's services at the Evanston Public Library. Ida Faye Wright and the school system's administrators were enthusiastic about this cooperative system and spoke and wrote about it. It had many features to recommend it.

Evanston was not alone in developing a cooperative school-and-public library service. Cleveland, Pittsburgh, and Seattle also had school library service in which the public library and the school system cooperated. In these cities, the high schools had school library rooms and a full-time staff. There were usually a few elementary school libraries with trained staff, too. Nor was Evanston the only smaller city library cooperating to provide elementary school library service. Brookline Public Library in Massachusetts cooperated with the elementary and high schools in such a program. There may have been others.

Ida Faye Wright's professional enthusiasm, her innovations, and her fine community relations made the years from 1928 to 1936 stimulating and rewarding for me. Added to that was the privilege of working with the outstanding Haven School principal, Helen M. Sanford (b. 1889). During those years I taught school library courses three summers at Indiana and Syracuse universities.

Late in 1935 I was offered and accepted the position of school library specialist in the ALA School and Children's Library Division then being established. When the division's chief, Jessie Gay Van Cleve (1880–1944) became ill and in the fall of 1937 had to resign, I became the chief and the only professional in the division for the remainder of the decade. The officers of the three ALA groups—the Section for Library Work with Children, the School Libraries Section, and the Young People's Reading Round Table—looked to the division for answers to their questions. The major responsibility of the division was to give information and advisory service in its fields, and for this, field trips supplemented by correspondence were very important. Trips were made in the late thirties to several larger cities to see public and school libraries. We also visited a number of states, where, traveling with state leaders, we saw outstanding experimental and typical programs in school and public library service to children and young people. There was a close relationship between the public library and the school system in some communities and almost none in others.

Before 1940 it became clear that the school library systems financed by public libraries with some board of education funding had served a very useful purpose as demonstrations in the twenties and early thirties. They showed how important school libraries are in a school program. But it was also becoming clear to me and others that this arrangement was not the right long-term answer. To be fully effective the school library had to be an integral part of the school's education program. That goal could be accomplished only when schools took complete responsibility for school libraries, for funding personnel, and for selection and organization of materials. Gradually this direction was taken, with the help of federal aid for school libraries and the availability of increasing numbers of trained school librarians during the next two decades.

Through the field trips and attendance at national library and education meetings (National Education Association, American Association of School Superintendents, National Council of Teachers of English, Association of Curriculum Development, Progressive Education Association, and others) as well as state library meetings in the twenties and thirties, it was evident that the number and quality of school libraries and of school librarians varied tremendously. So did the commitment of educators to school libraries. To be sure, the *Standards for Library Organization and Equipment for Secondary Schools*, edited by C. C. Certain, chairman of the Department of English in Detroit's Case High School, with Mary Hall (1874–1956), librarian at Girls High School in Brooklyn, as his chief collaborator, was published by the National Education Association (NEA) in 1918 and by ALA in 1920.[30] As valuable as the standards were, they had no force unless states or cities incorporated them into their enforced standards and this did not happen very rapidly in the 1920s and 1930s.

Progress was certainly being made, however, and across the nation there were a number of cities with excellent school libraries. I point with pride to Omaha Technical High School which, when I was in Omaha from 1924 to 1927, had a fine library with fine trained librarians and a fine program. Among strong school library systems it is not surprising to find that one was under the Detroit board of education.

Detroit schools in 1922 organized a department of school libraries with C. C. Certain as its director. That same year Marion Lovis (d. 1930), Simmons Library School 1909, became librarian of Detroit's Hutchins Intermediate School. In 1925 she succeeded Certain as supervisor of school libraries and held the position until her death in 1930. She was chairman of the ALA School Libraries Section in 1927–28 at the West Baden, Indiana, conference. The Detroit high schools and intermediate schools had libraries, and the "platoon" or "duplicate" system was planned for introducing libraries into the elementary schools. The plan was part of a new organization aimed at alleviating overcrowding resulting from rapid population growth in the city. In each platoon school, specialists in music, literature, science, and library service were added to the staff, and an auditorium, library, and gymnasium were provided. Implementation of the development of the elementary school libraries was Marion Lovis's most demanding task.

With 122 elementary schools, many librarians were needed. Training courses were organized under the supervision of Martha Caroline Pritchard (1882–1959), New York Public Library School 1913, who became librarian at Detroit Teachers College in 1920. Lovis was able to report that by 1928 Detroit had libraries in 87 elementary schools, 13 intermediate schools, 13 high schools, and 2 colleges under the Board of Education. Following Lovis's death, Dorotha Dawson (d. 1985), her assistant, was named acting supervisor, and in 1934 Lois Place was named supervisor.[31] When Jessie Van Cleve and I visited Detroit in 1936 the head of the public library children's department, Jessie Tompkins (1885–1949) and Lois Place arranged a combined meeting of children's and school librarians of the two institutions, a kind of meeting which until then had not been held.

The Los Angeles City Schools in 1920 employed Jasmine Britton, whose earlier career as a children's librarian has already been noted. Her position with the system was as supervisor of elementary libraries, textbooks, and audiovisual materials. In 1929 she became head supervisor of elementary, secondary, and junior college libraries. The development program she launched culminated in libraries in every elementary school in the fifties and sixties. The program was well on its way to completion in 1951 when she retired. Britton had a talent for inspiring staff and a genius for organization. She also had a facility for pleasant insistence, when presenting plans to authorities at various levels in seeking their support for added funds or new projects. Nationally as well as in California she was recognized as a leader.[32]

Two others on the department headquarters staff whose activities and influence reached well beyond Los Angeles were Marion Horton (1887–1984), who was in charge of selection and ordering of books and materials, and Elizabeth Williams (b. 1896), who was assistant supervisor of elementary libraries and textbooks from 1928 and who in 1951 succeeded Jasmine Britton as head supervisor.

From my first California visit as an ALA staff member in 1939 in advance of the ALA conference in San Francisco, I remember the Los Angeles librarians and also especially remember two others. Margaret Girdner (1893–1970) was supervisor of the San Francisco school libraries and a community leader in more than libraries. And Jewel Gardiner (1901–1956) supervised school libraries in Sacramento and would substitute for me at ALA one summer while I was teaching. With Leo B. Baisden, she wrote *Administering Library Service in Elementary Schools*, which was published by ALA in 1941.

One more California librarian, Jessie Boyd (1899–1978), was a person remembered by everyone who had contact with her. She was a friend and an inspiration to many. I think I first met her at the 1939 ALA conference. Over the years I very profitably sought her advice many times. Jessie Boyd was librarian at Fremont High School in Oakland from 1932 until 1935. In 1936 she became librarian at the University High School in Oakland, which was a practice school for the University of California School of Education, and thus was influential in teacher education. She remained on the staff there until 1947 and from that post exerted a significant influence on teachers' and school administrators' understanding of the importance school libraries have in teacher education. Reciprocally she helped school librarians to develop good relationships with teachers and other school personnel. In 1948 she was made director of Oakland school libraries and held that position until her retirement in 1963. It was especially her career at University High School and her lecturing during those years at the University of California in the schools of education and librarianship that made her influence so widespread.[33]

The Newark public school libraries were outstanding in the 1930s. Marguerite Kirk (b. 1894), Wisconsin Library School 1922, was appointed supervisor of school libraries and audiovisual services in 1929. She was one of the early librarians or school administrators to recognize the importance of evaluating, organizing, promoting, and distributing films, filmstrips, recordings, and other audiovisual materials in the same manner as books and integrated with them. At this period salesmen for audiovisual equipment dealt with school administrators, who seemed fascinated with the equipment. It was also true that many librarians did not reach out to include or even welcome audiovisual materials. The forward-looking Newark schools program was described by Kirk in *Educational Motion Pictures and Libraries* (ALA, 1942), edited by Gerald McDonald.

Those school and public library systems which early accepted or received responsibility for audiovisual materials had a considerable advantage in developing services that teachers and community members found responsive to their needs. They could make it readily possible to consider at one time in one place the best materials to serve teaching or individual needs.

In the two decades under consideration there was a significant increase in the number of state school library supervisors. By virtue of their positions, they were leaders, and their influence was considerable when they happened to be outstanding as people and as librarians as many of this period were. In a few states there were such supervisors in state education departments from 1920 on.

In the Minnesota Department of Public Instruction, Harriet Wood, the second school library supervisor in that state, held the position from 1919 to 1936. She was very active nationally chairing the ALA Education Committee from 1920 to 1929 and making it a major influence in school library progress during that period.[34] Five *School Library Yearbook*s were published under the committee's auspices by ALA from 1927 to 1932. In Minnesota Harriet Wood was concerned with stimulating teachers colleges to train school librarians so as to show teachers-in-training what school librarians could mean to teaching. It was Wood who persuaded St. Cloud Teachers College to add a children's librarian to the staff in 1927, the position she recruited me to pioneer when the college agreed to her proposal.

The New York State Education Department's school library supervisor was Sabra Vought (d. 1942) from 1919 to 1924. Then Vought became librarian for the U.S. Office of Education Library in Washington, D.C. Anna Clark Kennedy (1891–1984), a colleague in my New York State Library School class of 1923, became state supervisor in New York in 1929. In several visits to New York State school libraries with her, I learned much of the importance and problems of the enforcement of state standards in relation to steady school library growth. Good school libraries, especially at the junior high and high school level, were common, and quality elementary school libraries were becoming more usual in New York State by the end of the thirties.

Anna Kennedy was one of the outstanding leaders of the state school library supervisor's group over the years. In 1933–34 she was chairman of the ALA School Libraries Section. At the 1934 ALA conference in Montreal she was responsible for a dinner program honoring school library pioneers that those of us attending have long remembered. Present were:

Lucile Fargo (1880–1962), librarian at North Central High School in Spokane, Washington, from 1909 to 1926 and author of *The Library in the School* (ALA, 1930), one of the Library Curriculum Studies series. After serving on the ALA Headquarters staff from 1926 to 1928 on the Board of Education for Librarianship, Lucile Fargo taught at Peabody College School of Librarianship, at Columbia University School of Library Service, and at Western Reserve University Library School until her retirement in 1945.[35]

Clara Howard (1879–1935), librarian at Schenley High School, Pittsburgh, Pennsylvania, from 1916 to 1927. In 1928 she was named director of the New Jersey College for Women Library School, and from 1930 on served as dean of the Emory University Library School.

Martha Wilson (d. 1965), state school library supervisor in the Minnesota Department of Public Instruction from 1911 to 1919. She was succeeded by Harriet Wood. Martha Wilson went to the Lincoln Library in Springfield, Illinois, as librarian until 1940 or 1941.

Mary Davis (1881–1928), librarian of the Brookline High School, Massachusetts, from 1917 to 1929 and then librarian of the Medford Public Library, Massachusetts.

Mary Richardson (1880–1967), librarian at the New York State Normal School in Geneseo from 1906 to 1915 and 1917 to 1933.

Each talked about her early experiences. Most mentioned writing to Mary Hall (1864–1956) for help in starting their school libraries. In addition to the references to Mary Hall by the honorees, I remember that Margaret Greer (1891–1956), then supervisor of school libraries in Minneapolis, added from the audience that she had also written Mary Hall for help when starting her school library. It was unfortunate that Hall was not able to be at that celebration.

Mary Hall, Pratt 1895, was librarian at Girls' High School in Brooklyn from 1903 until her retirement in 1944. In 1910 she began what she was later to be called an "organized national campaign for better school libraries."

Mary Hall worked in the National Council of Teachers of English, the NEA, and the ALA for school library standards, joining forces with C. C. Certain, then chairman of the English Department at Cass High School in Detroit, who also devoted years to this goal. The resulting high school library standards were printed by NEA in 1918 and by ALA in 1920, but enforcement of any but local standards was to occur far in the future.[36] Hall was chairman of the ALA School Libraries Section in 1915, the year it was established. She was not able to attend the 1915 ALA conference in Berkeley, California, but she did attend the 1916 Asbury Park conference. When Mary Hall spoke at the 1924 Saratoga Springs ALA conference she repeated Mary Wright Plummer's prophecy that in ten years we would see great developments in the high school library. Indeed there had been progress but there would be much more widespread progress in the next three to four decades.

The Michigan State Library's school library supervisor from 1926 to 1929 was Lois Shortess (1895–1977), University of Illinois Library

School 1923. She was followed by Isabel Horne, University of Illinois 1922, who held the position through the 1940s. Louisiana was Lois Shortess's home state and when a state school library program was started there she became the supervisor in the Louisiana State Education Department, serving from 1929 to 1940. During this period Shortess, who was active in ALA, was a member of the ALA Board on Library Service to Children and Young People, which in the mid-thirties had taken the leadership in working for the establishment at ALA Headquarters of the School and Children's Library Division. The week-long Louisiana field trip Jessie Gay Van Cleve and I took in 1936 included two and sometimes three cars and was led by Lois Shortess and Essae Culver (1882–1973), director of the Louisiana State Library.

In Indiana, Helen M. Clark (b. 1900), University of Illinois 1927, was the school library adviser on the State Library's staff. Through her I was afforded the opportunity to teach school library courses at Indiana University in the early thirties. It was at her suggestion that I was made ALA School Libraries Section hospitality chairman for the 1933 ALA conference in Chicago during the Century of Progress exposition, an experience which led to many professional contacts and opportunities.

In the 1920s there was great concern about the need to improve education in the South. As part of a program made possible by grants from several foundations, the General Education Board (GEB) with Rockefeller (and perhaps other) funding established a program to improve school libraries in southern states. It provided funds to several states for the salary and travel expenses of a state school library supervisor for a period of years. Each state provided some funds for state aid to school libraries and committed itself to continue the program. Louisiana, where Shortess became supervisor, received help from the GEB program, as did those that follow. Other states were later added.

In the North Carolina Department of Public Instruction the state school library supervisor throughout the 1930s was Mary Peacock Douglas (1903–1970), Columbia University School of Library Service 1930. Mrs. Douglas developed a vigorous program and became very active in the ALA.

Martha Parks (1897–1980), University of Illinois 1927, went to Tennessee's state education department as school library supervisor and was there until 1945. Parks had been assistant state school library supervisor in New York from 1930 to 1932. She also was active in ALA.

Sarah Jones (b. 1902) became chief library consultant in the Georgia state education department, with responsibility for school libraries, in 1937 and served in that position into the 1960s.

This group of women, the state supervisors, were remarkable library leaders in the 1930s. Their positions at the state level helped them but more important was their tremendous and imaginative interest and planning for the growth of school libraries. They usually attended American Library Association conferences and shared their experiences, each thus enhancing her state's program. A state professional organization for school librarians was started early, in 1915, in California, and only three years later one was organized in New England.

The California School Library Association (CSLA) was founded by a group of eight school librarians who met during the National Education Association meeting in Oakland in 1915. Of the group I knew three in later years: Marjorie Van Deusen, Los Angeles; Marion Horton, then Oakland, later Los Angeles; and Elizabeth Madison (1883–1963), Oakland.

In its beginning years CSLA achieved a milestone for school library progress. State certification of school librarians was proposed and the support of educators was sought and received. In 1917 the governor signed the legislation. Previously, librarians had had to obtain teachers' certificates to qualify for salaries comparable to those of teachers. This act considerably increased the employment of professional librarians in California schools.

Because of the great distances in the state, the association was organized into a northern and a southern section, each meeting regularly. As membership grew, it was decided that the association would gain strength by having a statewide meeting annually. After a joint meeting of the sections in 1935, a new constitution was drawn up and the first annual state meeting occurred in 1936. The *Bulletin of the School Library Association of California* then became the responsibility of the state organization.[37]

The sections continued with their own officers, meetings, and activities. One of the most popular activities of the Southern Branch was the Book Breakfast. In a southern section folder called "Helping the School by Helping the Library," edited by Hope Potter, probably in the 1930s, Marjorie Van Deusen describes them:

> Time to read is as rare for school librarians as for any other busy persons yet read we must, not only for the breath of life, but also as part of the day's work in book selection. Book reviews help, but too often do not make clear the suitability of the book for a school library. And so we cooperate, exchanging with each other the results of our reading at a Book Breakfast.
>
> Book Breakfasts were inaugurated about eight years ago by the School Library Association, Southern Branch. The first Saturday of each month from 30 to 60 school librarians (and teachers too, if they will) gather in the pleasant lunch room of the Los Angeles Public Library for a 9 o'clock breakfast. After breakfast the morning is devoted to brief and lively reviews of new books from the school library standpoint. Usually 30 or 40 books are evaluated by 11 o'clock. Books for review at the next meeting, generously loaned by cooperating book stores and publishers, are distributed by the Book Committee. And finally annotated lists of the books reviewed are printed in the Association Bulletin reaching those who are too far away to come to the Breakfasts.

The New England School Library Association (NESLA) was established in 1918. The group of over a dozen who assembled in Brookline, Massachusetts, to organize it included five school librarians, Mary Hall among them, two librarians of public libraries, Alice Jordan, Boston Public Library children's librarian, two heads of high school English departments, two headmasters, who elsewhere would be high school or preparatory school principals, June Donnelly, director of the School of Library Science at Simmons, and Martha C. Pritchard (1862–1959), librarian at the Bridgewater Normal School (Massachusetts).[38] Martha Pritchard became the group's first president and June Donnelly, the second.[39] In the late thirties I came to know and work with some of NESLA's leaders, especially Edith Coulman (b. 1892), Quincy, Massachusetts, high school librarian, and Rheta Clark (b. 1902), Lyman Hall High School librarian, Wallingford, Connecticut. As a native New Englander, I found the several NESLA meetings I attended to be highlights.

Many state associations of school librarians began as sections of state library or teachers associations, and a few independent state school library associations came into existence in the thirties. By 1940 there were associations in thirty-nine states,[40] and from these would emerge the national leaders of the next decades.

YOUNG
PEOPLE'S
LIBRARIANS
AND SERVICES
IN PUBLIC
LIBRARIES

Young people of high school age in the twenties and thirties could be overwhelmed and discouraged by the large adult book collections when they first tried to use a public library's adult department. Some libraries helped in the transition by having in the children's department, near the adult department or in it, a collection of adult books, often in illustrated editions. At the Omaha Public Library in the mid-twenties we had in the children's department two cases of adult books, adding new adult titles to keep the collection inviting and fluid.

At about this time the Detroit Public Library added a new kind of position in its adult department, a reader's adviser.[41] Not long after, the Omaha Public Library added reader's advisers. They were popular with adults but also with young people who worked up the courage to approach them. The mid-twenties also brought the beginnings of public library services for young people.

When Anne Carroll Moore added Mabel Williams (b. 1887), Simmons 1909, to the New York Public Library's children's department staff in 1916, it was for work with schools. Class instruction and school reference work, however, were not to be program goals. Classes visiting the library were to be given "exposure to books and spirited talk about them by people who had read them and could excite interest in others. Book talks as a distinct . . . genre . . . became the subject of study, critical appraisal and analysis, recognized as arts in their own right."[42] These book talks were given in the library and in the schools.

Gradually, under Mabel Williams's leadership, special space for teenagers in branch libraries was provided just as it was for children. By 1924 Williams's work center had been moved from a desk in Anne Carroll Moore's office to an office of her own in the Fifty-eighth Street Branch. It was located on the second floor where, under her supervision, services for teachers were also provided. In 1930 Williams established the annual list *Books for the Teen Age* published by the New York Public Library. It was bought by libraries and teachers throughout the country, an annually revised, well-tested list which has continued to the present. Also in 1930 Mabel Williams was one of the founders of the ALA Young Peoples Reading Round Table and in 1935–36 was chairman for round table meetings at the 1936 Richmond conference of the ALA.

In 1926 Margaret Scoggin (1905–1968) joined the New York Public

Library staff of young people's librarians and, after spending 1929 at the University of London School of Librarianship, returned to New York Public Library young people's work for the rest of her distinguished career, retiring in 1967. She was the library's vocational school specialist. Chairman of the Young Peoples Reading Round Table during 1940–41, she presided at its meeting at the 1941 ALA conference in Boston.

Margaret Scoggin's cordial yet reserved relationship with young people, her great knowledge of books, and her talent for introducing books to groups as well as to individuals led many young people to discover the pleasure of reading. They felt she truly understood them and knew which books they would enjoy. It was these abilities which were the basis for her very successful weekly radio shows— and later television shows—on books, which she began in the forties. The show remained on the air into the 1960s. Participation of young people was a feature of her programs.

In the later decades Scoggin was involved in ALA international committees and projects. She was in Munich in 1948 for some weeks advising Jella Lepman (1890–1970), the founder of the International Youth Library (IYL), on its original organization. In 1969 in her honor the U.S. Children's Book Council (CBC) established the Margaret Scoggin Memorial Collection of Notable Children's and Young Adult Books.[43] From 1968 to 1982 publishers followed the CBC plan, annually sending to IYL all the children's books named as ALA Notable Children's Books and as Best Books for Young Adults. In 1970 the U.S. National Section of the International Board on Books for Young People (IBBY) began a further Scoggin project administered by the CBC and the ALA Children's Services Division's International Relations Committee. In the first year approximately fifteen titles were especially selected and sent to children's book collections in Ecuador, Ghana, Iran, Pakistan, Tanzania, and Venezuela. Six more sites were added in the next few years. This program continued until 1982.[44]

The Cleveland Public Library began giving attention to the library needs of young people in 1909 with the provision of a special shelf in the main library's fiction department. Filled with adult books, it was very popular, and while young people were not limited to this selection, it helped them locate books that would appeal to them. South Branch started an alcove for young people in its adult room in

1911 and Miles Park Branch began a special collection for young people in 1923.[45]

When the Cleveland Public Library opened its new main library building in 1925 it contained an entirely new public library feature: an attractive room for young people with its own staff under the direction of Jean C. Roos (1891–1982), Western Reserve 1928. Individual reading guidance of young people from fourteen to twenty was the department's aim from the beginning. Many ways of encouraging good reading were explored. Not only high school students but many out-of-school youth used the room. In addition it became a haven for youth workers, teachers, and parents.

One kind of help which the Stevenson Room staff believed would be most useful were book lists selected to represent the interests of young people at all levels of ability and which would lead them into the world of books with enthusiasm. To make these lists Jean Roos established committees including Stevenson Room staff, librarians from the high schools, and others. In 1931 one major list, *By Way of Introduction*, was published. It categorized and described 1,000 adult books. The list was revised and published in 1935 by ALA, and it was widely used across the country.

The Stevenson Room welcomed and assisted several groups of young people with special interests. There was a group for book discussions, another for poetry. The latter met weekly to write poems and to discuss what had been written. An adviser was provided by the Stevenson Room and a compilation of the poetry written by the group was attractively published as *Preludes to Poetry* and distributed by the Cleveland Public Library in 1931.

For the 1931 Conference of the ALA in New Haven, Roos was chairman of the round table, then in its second year of existence. Soon she became chairman of the ALA Board on Library Service to Children and Young People, the purpose of which was to seek ways that the many concerns of school, children's, and young people's librarians could be represented at ALA headquarters. The board under the chairmanship of Jean Roos persuaded the ALA Executive Board that staff representation was essential and in 1936 the School and Children's Library Division was established at ALA. As one of the two members of the new division staff, I was especially grateful to Jean Roos for her help to us in getting started in the early years.

That experience began a long and rewarding professional friendship for me.

At the 1940 White House Conference on Children in a Democracy, ALA's two official representatives were Jean Roos and the president of ALA, Ralph Munn, librarian of the Carnegie Library in Pittsburgh. Also in 1940 Roos was made supervisor of the youth department at the Cleveland Public Library, further extending her leadership responsibilities.

Work with young people at the Enoch Pratt Free Library in Baltimore began and was developed by Margaret Alexander (b. 1902) with imagination and enthusiasm. A Texan and a teacher of literature and Latin she came to Maryland originally as a teacher. She became a member of the Enoch Pratt Free Library adult department staff in 1933. She heard about the work with young people at the New York Public Library and visited Mabel Williams, who headed it, to observe the program. She was impressed with what she saw.

Soon Margaret Alexander suggested that she be designated a young people's librarian at the Pratt Library, and Joseph Wheeler, the director, gave her that appointment in 1936. She took home stacks of books to read. Located in a corner of the Popular Library, she found young people eager for help. With her extensive book knowledge and her understanding of young people's interests she usually came up with "just the right book." Those readers came back for more, and told friends of the young people's librarian who really could find the best books. She gave book talks to high school classes and groups elsewhere, lively dynamic talks which stimulated young people and their teachers to find reading exciting.

Gradually more young people's librarians were added to the staff at the central library and in branches. Margaret Alexander made sure they knew and were enthusiastic about books young people would like and knew how to share books with them. Each new young people's librarian had to read 200 books—or perhaps it was 300— and report on them to her. Librarians who were to work with teenagers were trained to give book talks. After observing talks by experienced librarians, they prepared and gave one or more book talks which were critiqued by Alexander until the talks were accepted as up to standard. It was no easy task to achieve the level of accomplishment she required, but the rewards to the young librarians who went through this regimen and had experience on that staff were personally as well as professionally invaluable. Each had developed a wealth of book knowledge and skills for sharing books. There were no special rooms for young people for it was Alexander's philosophy that young people should have the run of the whole library's collections.

Margaret Alexander became Mrs. Edwards in 1944. She continued her vigorous and inspiring career and in 1949 was made coordinator of work with young people at the Pratt Library.[46] She had been chairman of the round table during 1939–40, presiding at the ALA Cincinnati conference in 1940. She wrote articles and books describing her approach to young people's (later called young adult) service. Her entire library career was spent at the Enoch Pratt Free Library. She retired in 1962.

Sarah Beard (1902–1984), Brooklyn Public Library Training Class 1925 and Columbia 1943, was a children's librarian from 1925 to 1927 at the Brooklyn Public Library. She was a children's librarian at the Ridgewood Public Library in New Jersey from 1927 to 1929. And in 1930 she returned to Brooklyn's Brownsville Library, a very busy branch limited to services to children and young people. It opened its second floor as a young people's room with Sarah Beard in charge from 1930 to 1941.[47] She was head of young people's work for the entire system from 1941 to 1943 and chairman of the Young People's Reading Round Table in 1941–42, when the last ALA conference before the wartime hiatus was held in Milwaukee.

Leaving Brooklyn for the Kansas City Public Library, she headed young people's work there during 1944–45. Then she combined her several kinds of experience in a position with the Massachusetts Department of Education as consultant for school libraries and public library work with children and young people.

By the mid-thirties staff to work with young adults were being hired in a number of smaller libraries as well as in an increasing number of large cities. Alice Louise Le Fevre (1898–1963), Columbia 1933, went to New Rochelle Public Library in New York in 1936 as a young people's librarian and was there until 1938. In 1936–37 she was chairman of the round table for the ALA conference in New York City in 1937. She had previously had experience as a school librarian in Cleveland and was an assistant at the ALA Board of Education for Librarianship in Chicago in 1926. Following the 1923

116

C. C. Williamson report, *Training for Library Service,* the ALA was facilitating the move to academic institutions of the training programs housed in public libraries and elsewhere. The board was also working on standards for training, which the report had found nonexistent. Training programs were found to vary from excellent to inadequate. In 1938 Le Fevre left young people's work for the education of librarians, well prepared by her background in school libraries and young people's work to lead in these fast-growing fields. She taught at the University of North Carolina in 1938–39 and at St. John's University, Jamaica, New York, from 1939 to 1945. Then she moved to Kalamazoo, Michigan, where she organized the Western Michigan University School of Librarianship, serving as the first director from 1945 to 1963. She was an ideal person to head such a program. Besides the appropriate background, she had an unusual talent for working with people, she had patience, and she had a wonderful sense of humor.

Sara Fenwick (b. 1908), Western Reserve 1931, went the year she graduated to the Wilkes Barre Public Library in Pennsylvania as an assistant children's librarian. In 1936 she became the library's young people's librarian, continuing in that position until 1941.

Returning to children's work by heading the department at Wilkes Barre from 1941 to 1944, Sara Fenwick then went to Baltimore's Enoch Pratt Free Library as assistant to Mary Wilkinson, director of the children's department there. In 1946 she moved to Indiana to head the Gary Public Library's children's department, and from there to Chicago in 1949 to become librarian at the Elementary School Laboratory School at the University of Chicago. Later she joined the faculty of the university's Graduate Library School, and she was a leader in the school library and children's library fields until her retirement in 1974.

Eleanor Kidder (b. 1907), University of Washington Library School 1929, began her career as a children's librarian at the Brooklyn Public Library in 1929. Three years later she moved to Ogden, Utah, where she became a junior high school librarian, and from there she moved to Indiana to work as a children's librarian at the Mishawaka Public Library. She entered young people's library service in 1936 when she was named head of work with young people for the Rochester Public Library in New York. She was chairman of the Young People's Reading Round Table in 1937–38, presiding at the 1938

ALA Kansas City conference. Eleanor Kidder moved to Seattle Public Library in 1944 and headed services to youth there until her retirement in the early seventies.

CONCLUSION   Librarians who work with children and young people are expected to be creative and empathetic and of course they are. I conclude with two of the poems written by a children's librarian, Inger Boye (b. 1896) of the Highland Park Public Library in Illinois. In 1957 the board of trustees of that library presented her with a beautifully printed booklet of the poems with which she had prefaced her annual reports from 1936 through the next twenty years.[48]

Here is the 1937 poem:

> A soul of a child
> Is like a Tapestry
> Of finely woven threads.
>
> If we may be the Weavers
> Oh, give us then the Shuttles
> And let us see the golden Threads.

And the one for 1939:

> Life is full of things we do not know
> Of Opportunities unused
> Of friendly thoughts well hidden
> Of feelings never worded
> Of big and little things
> Of values never recognized
>
> In books are secret doors
> Which may well open up
> To worlds of unknown richness.
> How much we help,
> How far we reach,
> We cannot know!
> But deep within our hearts
> A wish—a hope
> That we may help a child
> To glimpse the greater vistas.

NOTES

Dates mentioned have come chiefly from *Who's Who in Library Service*, editions of 1933, 1943, 1955, and 1966, supplemented by considerable correspondence, not all of it fruitful.

1. Jennie D. Lindquist, "Caroline Hewins and Her Books," in *The Hewins Lectures, 1947–1962* (Boston: Horn Book, Inc., 1963), 67–82.
2. Robert A. Karlowich and Nassar Sharify, "Mary Wright Plummer," in *Dictionary of American Library Biography* (Littleton, Colo.: Libraries Unlimited, 1978).
3. Frances Clarke Sayers, *Anne Carroll Moore* (New York: Atheneum, 1972), pp. 57, 62–63.
4. Anne Carroll Moore, "First Chairman Salutes C.L.A.," *Top of the News* 6 (May 1950): 5–6.
5. J. F. Ziff, "A Portrait of a Forgotten Pioneer: Lutie Eugenia Stearns (1866–1943)," an unpublished paper dated August 1, 1983.
6. Laura Grotzinger, "Katharine Lucinda Sharp," in *ALA World Encyclopedia of Library and Information Services* (Chicago: American Library Association, 1980).
7. Miriam A. Wessel, "Children's Library Association: Highlights of the Fifty Year History," *Top of the News* 6 (May 1950): 8–10.
8. American Library Association, *Papers and Proceedings*, Waukesha Conference (1901), p. 163.
9. Velmai Fenster, "Library Education at Madison, University of Wisconsin Library School," *Wisconsin Library Bulletin*, November–December 1975, 332.
10. Grotzinger, "Sharp."
11. Elva S. Smith, "As It Was in the Beginning—Frances Jenkins Olcott," *Public Libraries* 25 (October 1920): 417–20.
12. Frances Jenkins Olcott, "Rational Library Work with Children and the Preparation for It," *Library Journal* 30:74–75. Conference papers from September 1905. Elva S. Smith, "Carnegie Library School—A Bit of History," *Library Journal* 46 (October 1, 1921): 791–94.
13. Wessel, "Children's Library Association."
14. Letter from Tobbitt to MLB, June 19, 1924.
15. Sayers, *Anne Carroll Moore*, 62–79.
16. Letter from Priscilla Edie Morton to MLB, September 10, 1984.
17. Alice M. Jordan, "Forty Years of the Round Table of Children's Librarians," in *New England Round Table of Children's Librarians Handbook* (1968), 3–7. (Archives of the roundtable are in the Boston Public Library's Alice M. Jordan Collection.)
18. Linda J. Brass, *Eighty Years of Service: A History of the Children's Department of Seattle Public Library* (Seattle: Seattle Public Library, 1971).
19. Letter from Rosemary Livsey to MLB, October 25, 1984.
20. Effie L. Power, "To My Co-Workers," *Top of the News* 6 (May 1950): 7.
21. Effie L. Power, unpublished biographical material gathered by Alice Martin for the fiftieth anniversary of children's work in Cleveland, October 23, 1948.
22. Letter from Livsey to MLB, October 25, 1984.
23. Power, "To My Co-Workers."

24. Letter from Mary Wilkinson to MLB, February 22, 1983.
25. Ibid.
26. Mary Wilkinson, "The Enoch Pratt Free Library—As I Saw It," unpublished paper dated 1927.
27. Margaret E. Johnston, "Lillian H. Smith," *Horn Book Magazine* 58 (June 1982): 325–32.
28. Buffalo Public Library Annual Reports, 1905–9.
29. Elizabeth Gray Vining, "May Massee: Who Was She?" in *May Massee Collection, Creative Publishing for Children, 1923–1963* (Emporia, Kansas: William Allen White Library, Emporia State University, 1979), v.
30. Patricia Pond, "History of AASL, Part I; Origins and Developments, 1896–1951," in *School Library Media Annual* (Littleton, Colo.: Libraries Unlimited, 1983), 118.
31. Ruth Marie Edberg, *The Dynamic Evolution: A History of Detroit School Librarians, 1886–1962* (Detroit, Mich.: Board of Education, 1962).
32. Letters from Elizabeth Williams to MLB, October 20, 1984, March 20, 1985, and April 1, 1985.
33. Thelma C. Dahlin, "Jessie Boyd," *Bulletin of the School Library Association of California,* undated.
34. Pond, "History of AASL," 121.
35. "Lucile Foster Fargo (1880–1962)," in *Dictionary of American Library Biography* (Littleton, Colo.: Libraries Unlimited, 1978).
36. Pond, "History of AASL," 113–131; "Mary Evelyn Hall," in *Dictionary of American Library Biography* (Littleton, Colo.: Libraries Unlimited, 1978).
37. Hope L. Potter, "The S.L.A.C.—Past and Future," *Bulletin of the School Library Association of California,* May 1953.
38. Mary M. Pike and Mary D. Bair, *NESLA—A History of the New England School Library Association, 1918–1968* (The Association, 1968).
39. "Martha Pritchard (1882–1959)," in *Dictionary of American Library Biography* (Littleton, Colo.: Libraries Unlimited, 1978).
40. "Library Service for Youth in a Democracy: Eighth Annual Report of the Board on Library Service to Children and Young People," *ALA Bulletin* 34 (September 1940): 538.
41. Frank B. Woodford, *Parnassus on Main Street; A History of the Detroit Public Library* (Detroit, Mich.: Wayne State University Press, 1965), 258.
42. "Mabel Williams," in *ALA Yearbook* (Chicago: American Library Association, 1981), 79.
43. Children's Book Council, press release on the Scoggin Memorial Collection, dated April 1969.
44. Letter from John Donovan to MLB, May 31, 1985.
45. Anna Margaret Winings, "A Study of the Development of Work with Young People in the Cleveland Public Library," unpublished paper for Master of Science degree in Library Science, School of Library Science, Western Reserve University, June 1952.
46. Beverly Rubenstein, "Margaret Edwards, Mentor," *The Crab* 15 (March 1985): 9–10.
47. Letter from Sarah Beard to MLB, October 14, 1979.
48. Inger Boye, *Poems: 1936–1956* (Highland Park, Ill.: Highland Park Public Library, 1957).

THE SPEAKERS

*

SELECTED BIBLIOGRAPHY

*

SYMPOSIUM PARTICIPANTS

*

INDEX

THE SPEAKERS

*

MILDRED BATCHELDER, long a respected leader in children's librarianship, held a number of key positions with the American Library Association during her career. Among the several awards she has received are the Grolier Award of the American Library Association (1966) and the Constance Lindsay Skinner Award of the Women's National Book Association (1967). She retired in 1966. Since 1968, the Mildred L. Batchelder Award for the best translation of a foreign-language children's book has been given annually in her honor by the Children's Services Division of ALA. She is the subject of a dissertation by Dorothy J. Anderson entitled "Mildred L. Batchelder: A Study in Leadership" (Ph.D. diss., Texas Woman's University, 1981).

ABE LERNER, a noted book designer, has had a distinguished career in printing and design. Starting in publishing at Simon and Schuster in 1928, he later worked as assistant production manager at the Viking Press, 1937–42, then served as art director and production manager for the World Publishing Company, 1942–50 and 1954–63, and as director of design and production at the Macmillan Company, 1963–74. He worked with both May Massee and Velma Varner and has designed such classic picture books as James Daugherty's *Andy and the Lion* (1938), Robert McCloskey's *Make Way for Ducklings* (1941), and William Pène Du Bois's *The Three Policemen* (1938). Many of his books have been selected for Fifty Books of the Year exhibitions by the American Institute of Graphic Arts, and in 1955 he was chairman of the Fifty Books of the Year Committee. Currently Mr. Lerner is a free-lance book designer. He is president of the Typophiles and has edited, designed, and produced chapbooks and a new series of monographs for that organization.

ANNE MACLEOD is an associate professor at the University of Maryland College of Library and Information Services, where she was a Distinguished Scholar-Teacher in 1979–80. She specializes in the cultural significance of children's literature. She is the author of *A Moral Tale: Children's Fiction and American Culture, 1820–1860* (Hamden, Conn.: Archon Books, 1976).

JOHN TEBBEL, who has written a number of notable books on the media, is the author of the four-volume work *A History of Book Publishing in the United States*

(New York: R. R. Bowker, 1972–81), *The Media in America* (New York: Crowell, 1974), *The Press and Presidency* (New York: Oxford University Press, 1985), and *Between Covers* (New York: Oxford University Press, 1987). Mr. Tebbel was chairman of the New York University Department of Journalism from 1954 to 1965, serving for the following decade as professor of journalism in that department.

SYMPOSIUM PARTICIPANTS

*

Dorothy Anderson, Librarian, Los Angeles, California

Sharon Angus, Librarian, Dover, Delaware

Barbara Atkinson, Reading Is Fundamental, Washington, D.C.

Diane Barlow, University of Maryland, College Park, Maryland

Rosemary Zibart Barrow, *Washington Times*, Washington, D.C.

Barbara Bates, Editor, Children's Books, Westminster Press, Philadelphia, Pennsylvania

Mary Bauer, Prince George's County Memorial Library System, Hyattsville, Maryland

Ruth Boorstin, Washington, D.C.

Esther Wood Brady, Author, Washington, D.C.

Dale Brown, Educational Media Center, Alexandria, Virginia

Helen Canfield, Librarian Emerita, Hartford, Connecticut

Dudley B. Carlson, Librarian, Princeton, New Jersey

Josephine S. Carr, Writer, Alexandria, Virginia

Mary Childs, Director Emerita, Children's Book Council, Washington, D.C.

Rheta Clark, Librarian Emerita, S. Glastonbury, Connecticut

John Y. Cole, Center for the Book, Library of Congress

Mary Silva Cosgrave, Editor Emerita, Pocasset, Massachusetts

Margaret N. Coughlan, Children's Literature Center, Library of Congress

Ellis Credle, Writer, Jalisco, Mexico

John Donovan, Executive Director, Children's Book Council, New York, New York

MaryBeth Dunhouse, Alice M. Jordan Collection, Boston Public Library, Boston, Massachusetts

Julia Edwards, World Affairs Bureau, Washington, D.C.

Dilys Evans, Lucas-Evans Books, New York, New York

Carolyn W. Field, Children's Coordinator Emerita, Free Library of Philadelphia, Philadelphia, Pennsylvania

Howard Fields, *Publishers Weekly*, Washington, D.C.

Joanna Foster, Director Emerita, Children's Book Council, Westport, Connecticut

Patricia Francis, University of Maryland, College Park, Maryland

James H. Fraser, Editor, *Phaedrus*, Madison, New Jersey

Judy Furash, General Reading Rooms Division, Library of Congress

Barbara Geyger, Chief, Children's Division, Martin Luther King Memorial Library, Washington, D.C.

James Gilreath, Rare Book and Special Collections Division, Library of Congress

Delia Goetz, Writer, Washington, D.C.

Gail Haley, Artist, Boone, North Carolina

Jane Hannigan, Columbia University, New York, New York

Barbara Harrison, Center for the Study of Children's Literature, Boston, Massachusetts

Michael Patrick Hearn, Writer, New York, New York

Ethel Heins, Editor Emerita, *Horn Book Magazine*, Boston, Massachusetts

Paul Heins, Editor Emeritus, *Horn Book Magazine*, Boston, Massachusetts

Susan Hirschman, Editor, Greenwillow Books, New York, New York

Grace Allen Hogarth, Editor Emerita, London, England

Elizabeth Hoke, Coordinator, Children's Services, Montgomery County Public Library, Bethesda, Maryland

Anne Izard, Children's Librarian Emerita, Gwynedd, Pennsylvania

Sybille A. Jagusch, Chief, Children's Literature Center, Library of Congress

Virginia Kahl, Writer, Alexandria, Virginia

Jean Karl, Atheneum Books, New York, New York

Amy Kellman, Children's Coordinator, Carnegie Library of Pittsburgh, Pittsburgh, Pennsylvania

Gordon Kelly, Department of American Studies, University of Maryland, College Park, Maryland

Paul Koda, Catholic University of America, Washington, D.C.

Selma Lanes, Critic and Writer, New York, New York

Nancy Larrick, Writer, Winchester, Virginia

Suzanne Levesque, Children's Literature Center, Library of Congress

Barbara Lucas, Executive Director, Lucas-Evans Books, New York, New York

Margaret Maloney, The Osborne Collection, Toronto Public Library, Toronto, Canada

Robert McCloskey, Artist and Writer, Little Deer Isle, Maine

Margaret K. McElderry, Editor, Margaret K. McElderry Books, New York, New York

Bernard McTigue, Arents Collection, The New York Public Library, New York, New York

Carolyn Michaels, Librarian, Charleston County Public Library, Charleston, South Carolina

Barbara Moody, Children's Coordinator, Enoch Pratt Free Library, Baltimore, Maryland

Effie Lee Morris, Children's Coordinator Emerita, San Francisco Public Library, San Francisco, California

Angeline Moscatt, Central Children's Room, New York Public Library, New York, New York

Marguerite Murray, Children's Coordinator Emerita, Montgomery County Public Library, Garrett Park, Maryland

Greenie Neuburg, Cheshire Cat Bookstore, Washington, D.C.

Lucille Ogle, Editor Emerita, New York, New York

Dana Pratt, Director, Publishing Office, Library of Congress

Harriet B. Quimby, Professor Emerita, St. John's University, West Falmouth, Massachusetts

Winifred Ragsdale, Children's Book Specialist, Altadena, California

Selma K. Richardson, University of Illinois, Champaign, Illinois

Mae Durham Roger, University of California at Berkeley, Mill Valley, California

Mary June Roggenbuck, Catholic University of America, Washington, D.C.

Maria Salvadore, Coordinator, Children's Services, Martin Luther King Memorial Library, Washington, D.C.

Alice Schreyer, Center for the Book, Library of Congress

Mirian Sealfon, Librarian, Philadelphia, Pennsylvania

Frances V. Sedney, Coordinator, Children's Services, Hartford County Library, Bel Air, Maryland

Tayo Shima, Consulting Editor, Washington, D.C.

Anita Silvey, Editor, *Horn Book Magazine*, Boston, Massachusetts

Evelyn Sinclair, Publishing Office, Library of Congress

Sharyl G. Smith, Librarian, New York, New York

Judith St. John, Director Emerita, The Osborne Collection, Toronto Public Library, Toronto, Canada

Jewell Stoddard, Cheshire Cat Bookstore, Washington, D.C.

Kay Vandergrift, Columbia University, New York, New York

Barbara Van Hook, Abingdon, Pennsylvania

Ann Weeks, Association for Library Service to Children, American Library Association, Chicago, Illinois

Eva Weiss, Art Director, Greenwillow Books, New York, New York

Hazel Wilson, Writer, Bethesda, Maryland

Charlotte Zolotow, Editor, Harper Junior Books Group, New York, New York

SELECTED BIBLIOGRAPHY

*

Listed in this bibliography are children's books from the
twenties and thirties mentioned in the preceding essays.
For most authors and illustrators discussed,
life dates have been provided here.

ARMER, LAURA ADAMS (1874–1963). *Waterless Mountain.* New York and Toronto: Longmans, Green, and Co., 1931.

ARTZYBASHEFF, BORIS (1899–1965). *Seven Simeons: A Russian Tale.* New
York: The Viking Press, 1937.

ASHMUN, MARGARET (1875–1940). *Mother's Away.* New York: The Macmillan Co., 1927.

BANNERMAN, HELEN (1863?–1946). *Little Black Sambo.* New York: Platt &
Munk Co., 1933.

BIANCO, MARGERY WILLIAMS (1881–1944). *The Velveteen Rabbit; or, How
Toys Become Real.* Illustrated by William Nicholson. New York: G. H.
Doran Co., 1922.

BOYD, JAMES (1888–1944). *Drums.* Illustrated by N. C. Wyeth. New York:
C. Scribner's Sons, 1928.

BURTON, VIRGINIA LEE (1909–1968). *The Little House.* Boston: Houghton
Mifflin, 1942.

BUTLER, ELLIS PARKER (1869–1937), and Louise A. Kent (b. 1886). *Jo Ann,
Tomboy.* Boston: Houghton Mifflin, 1933.

BYRD, RICHARD EVELYN (1888–1957). *Skyward.* New York: Putnam; London:
Knickerbocker Press, 1928.

CALDWELL, ERSKINE (b. 1903). *Georgia Boy.* New York: Duell, Sloan and
Pearce, 1943; Cleveland: World Publishing Co., [1944].

CASSERLY, ANN (1851–1974). *Michael of Ireland.* London: Faber and Gwyer,
1926; New York: Harper & Bros., 1927.

CHRISMAN, ARTHUR B. (1889–1953). *Shen of the Sea.* Illustrated by Else Has-
selbriis (b. 1877). New York: E. P. Dutton, 1925.

COATSWORTH, ELIZABETH JANE (1893–1986). *Alice-All-by-Herself.* Illustrated by Marguerite De Angeli. New York: The Macmillan Co., 1937.

COBB, BERTHA B. (1867–1951), and Ernest Cobb (b. 1877). *Dan's Boy.* Illustrated by S. J. Bridgman. Newton Upper Falls, Mass.: The Arlo Publishing
Co., 1926.

DAUGHERTY, JAMES (1889–1974). *Andy and the Lion.* New York: The Viking
Press, 1938.

Du bois, william pène (b. 1916). *The Three Policemen: Or, Young Bottsford of Farbe Island.* New York: The Viking Press, 1938.

Eaton, jeanette (1886–1968). *A Daughter of the Seine: The Life of Madame Roland.* New York and London: Harper and Brothers, 1929.

Eberle, irmengarde (1898–1979). *Spice on the Wind.* Illustrated by Richard Jones. New York: Holiday House, 1940.

Edwards, leo, *pseud.*; see Lee, Edward Edson (1884–1944)

Enright, elizabeth (1909–1968). *Thimble Summer.* New York: Holt, Rinehart & Winston, 1938.

Estes, eleanor (b. 1906). *The Moffats.* Illustrated by Louis Slobodkin. New York: Harcourt Brace and Co., 1941.

Falls, c. b. (1874–1960). *ABC Book.* Garden City, N.Y.: Doubleday, Page, & Co., 1923.

Field, rachel (1894–1942). *Hitty, Her First Hundred Years.* New York: The Macmillan Co., 1929.

Finger, charles (1869–1941). *Tales from Silver Lands.* Woodcuts by Paul Honoré. Garden City, N.Y.: Doubleday, Page, & Co., 1924.

Fish, helen dean (1889–1953). *Animals of the Bible.* New York: Frederick A. Stokes, 1937.

Flack, marjorie (1899–1958), and Kurt Wiese (1887–1974). *The Story about Ping.* New York: The Viking Press, 1933.

Forbes, esther (1891–1967). *Johnny Tremain.* Boston: Houghton, Mifflin, 1943.

Gag, wanda (1893–1946). *Millions of Cats.* New York: Coward-McCann, 1928.

Gates, doris (b. 1901). *Blue Willow.* New York: The Viking Press, 1940.

Handforth, thomas (1897–1948). *Mei Li.* New York: Doubleday, Doran & Co., 1938.

Hawes, charles b. (1889–1923). *The Dark Frigate.* Boston: The Atlantic Monthly Press, c. 1923.

Hodgins, eric (b. 1899), and F. Alexander Magoun (b. 1896). *Sky High: The Story of Aviation.* Boston: Little, Brown, and Co., 1929.

James, will (1892–1942). *Smoky, the Cowhorse.* New York and London: C. Scribner's Sons, 1926.

Jope-slade, christine (b. 1893). *St. David Walks Again.* Illustrated by Eleanor Parke Custis. New York and London: Harper & Brothers, 1928.

Keene, carolyn, *pseud. The Hidden Staircase.* Illustrated by Russell H. Tandy. New York: Grosset & Dunlap, c. 1930.

Kelly, eric p. (1884–1960). *The Trumpeter of Krakow, a Tale of the Fifteenth Century.* Illustrated by Angela Pruszynska. New York: The Macmillan Co., 1928.

Lagerlöf, selma (1858–1940). *The Wonderful Adventure of Nils.* Translated from the Swedish by Velma Swanston Howard. New York: Doubleday, Doran, 1938, c. 1907.

Lawson, robert (1892–1957). *Rabbit Hill.* New York: The Viking Press, 1944.

LEAF, MUNRO (1905–1976). *The Story of Ferdinand.* Illustrated by Robert Lawson. New York: The Viking Press, 1936.

LEE, EDWARD EDSON (1884–1944). *Jerry Todd and the Bob-Tailed Elephant.* By Lee Edwards (*pseud.*). Illustrated by Bert Salg. New York: Grosset & Dunlap, 1929.

LINDSAY, NICHOLAS VACHEL (1879–1931). *Johnny Appleseed, and Other Poems.* Illustrated by George Richards. New York: The Macmillan Co., 1928.

LOFTING, HUGH (1886–1947). *The Voyages of Doctor Dolittle.* New York: Frederick A. Stokes, 1922.

McCLOSKEY, ROBERT (b. 1914). *Make Way for Ducklings.* New York: The Viking Press, 1941.

MacGOWAN, ALICE (1858–1947). *A Girl of the Plains Country.* New York: Frederick Stokes Co., 1924.

MILNE, A. A. (1882–1956). *When We Were Very Young.* New York: E. P. Dutton & Co., 1924.

MUKERJI, DHAN GOPAL (1890–1936). *Hindu Fables for Little Children.* Illustrated by Kurt Wiese. New York: E. P. Dutton & Co., 1929.

PETERSHAM, MAUD FULLER (1890–1971), and Miska Petersham (b. 1888). *The Rooster Crows: A Book of American Rhymes and Jingles.* New York: The Macmillan Co., 1945.

PIER, ARTHUR (1874–1966). *David Ives: A Story of St. Timothy's.* Illustrated by Franklin Wood. Boston: Houghton Mifflin Co., 1922.

PIPER, WATTY, *pseud.* (1870–1945). *The Little Engine That Could.* Illustrated by Lois Lenski (b. 1893). New York: The Platt & Munk Co., 1930.

PLOWHEAD, RUTH GIPSON (1877–1967). *Josie and Joe.* Illustrated by Marguerite De Angeli. Caldwell, Idaho: Caxton Printers, 1938.

PRICE, EDITH BALLINGER (b. 1897). *John and Susanne.* New York and London: The Century Co., 1926.

RICHARDS, LAURA HOWE (1850–1943). *Star Bright.* Illustrated by Frank T. Merrill. Boston: L. C. Page & Co., 1927.

ROBERTS, ELIZABETH MADOX (1886–1941). *Under the Tree.* New York: B. W. Huebsch, 1922.

ROBINSON, MABEL L. (1882?–1962). *All by Ourselves.* Illustrated by Mary Sherwood Wright. New York: E. P. Dutton, 1924.

ROBINSON, THOMAS PENDLETON (b. 1878). *Buttons.* Illustrated by Peggy Bacon (1895–1987). New York: The Viking Press, 1938.

ROOSEVELT, THEODORE (1858–1919). *Diaries of Boyhood and Youth.* New York and London: Charles Scribner's Sons, 1928.

ROUNDS, GLEN (b. 1906). *Lumbercamp.* New York: Holiday House, 1937.

SANDBURG, CARL (1878–1967). *Abe Lincoln Grows Up.* Illustrated by James Daugherty. New York: Harcourt, Brace & Co., 1928.

SEREDY, KATE (1899–1975). *The White Stag.* New York: The Viking Press, 1937.

SUESS, DR., *pseud.* (b. 1904). *And to Think That I Saw It on Mulberry Street.* New York: Vanguard Press, 1937.

——. *The 500 Hats of Bartholomew Cubbins.* New York: Vanguard Press, 1938.

THURBER, JAMES (1894–1961). *Many Moons.* Illustrated by Louis Slobodkin. New York: Harcourt Brace, 1943.

VAN LOON, HENDRIK WILLEM (1882–1944). *The Story of Mankind.* New York: Boni and Liveright, 1921.

VILLIERS, ALAN JOHN (b. 1903). *Falmouth for Orders: The Story of the Last Clipper Ship Race around Cape Horn.* New York: H. Holt & Co., 1929.

VINING, ELIZABETH GRAY (b. 1902). *Adam of the Road.* Illustrated by Robert Lawson. New York: The Viking Press, 1942.

INDEX

*

133